GOD IS SPEAKING

are you listening?

ENCOURAGING WORDS FOR US

LYNNIE LANG

God Is Speaking,

ISBN
978-1-958122-28-0 (Paperback)
978-1-958122-27-3 (eBook)

Dedicated To

God, who gave me the gift to write and
encourage others to know He loves them,
and desires to speak through different channels the
truth and messages of His Word, the BIBLE.

CONTENTS

ACKNOWLEDGEMENTS

MY FAMILY AND friends who encouraged, loved, and tolerated me through changes needed from me to accomplish God's purpose and plans throughout my life.

Andrea, wonderful friend ever since I moved to Florida; who always knows when I am in need of something important in my life as God leads her to help it come to pass. She has an open heart to help others in many ways. A true friend in Christ in deed.

My Baby Sister, Dee, as she gets excited for me when God is moving in my life in a special way, and helps make things possible as God leads her.

My dear friend of many years, Prudy, who has always 'been there' to encourage me to keep on with the things God calls me to accomplish.

Another great friend, Patsy, who used her God given talents with ideas for the cover.

My young friend, Jamie, who treats me like her mom, and cared enough to give me her time and assistance in preparing everything the publisher needed me to send them.

All those who have gotten to read or hear these writings in different ways as God led, and continued to encourage me by asking when they were going to be in a book.

With heartfelt gratitude I mention the folks above, for I love them all dearly and am so blessed to have them and many others in my life.

1 Chronicles 28:9

"...Know thou the God of thy father, and serve Him with a perfect heart and with a willing mind: for the Lord searcheth all hearts, and understandeth all the imaginations of the thought: if thou seek Him, He will be found of thee..."

A FIRM FOUNDATION

When there is nothing between you and Me;
I will always hear when you call.
Totally rely on Me, and I will be here to speak
words of wisdom and guidance to you.
Always remember, your path is already ordered by the Lord.
Your life is hid in Christ, so you will glorify Me
in all that you do; yet you must continually yield to My will.
Circumstances and situations in this life
will always try to deter your focus away from me.
Be careful to not allow anything to keep you
from Me and My purpose for you.
Faithfully and continually come to Me for direction.
Watch out for the small insignificant stuff that will try to entrap you.
Remember, what matters most is what I have called you to do.
You are My disciple, keep your life disciplined in the things of God.
Meditate on My Word day and night, so you will have
the words to speak at all times.
Whenever you call on Me, I will answer.
For My people know Me and hear My voice;
but you must be attentive and obedient.
Always diligent in seeking and fulfilling the high calling in Christ Jesus,
which I have commissioned to all who fully commit and humble themselves
before Me.

Ephesians 6:10

"Finally be strong in the Lord and in the power of His might. put on the full armor of God, that ye may be able to stand against the wiles of the devil."

A LIFE HID IN CHRIST

Ah yes, complaining and arguing over the smallest of issues.
Think about it, things of this world are so very insignificant.
I, more than anything, desire you to let go of
these things that cause derision. I will help you.
Seek to be focused on the things that will build
a firm foundation in Me.
You must dislike the behavior that not being submitted causes.
Be sensitive to what and how people speak to you.
It is true human nature wants what it wants, when it wants it.
This, of course, is not good; unless it is lined
up with My Word.
So you see, even the small insignificant stuff must be considered.
For it is in those times that the spirit and
the flesh war against each other.
The prophet is always subject to the spirit.
This calls for self-control, a fruit of the Spirit.
You must engage this virtue for it to be effective.
If self in on the throne it will always want
dominion, but when you engage in
self-control, the Spirit within you will bringforth right behavior.
The flesh is weak, but the spirit is strong when
My Spirit resides there.
Walk in the Spirit, so you won't fulfill the lusts of the flesh.
Put others first always, as I did.
You are a servant of the Most High God.
Others think they are right even if they are not,
for I am the One Who will let them see
their faults, when they are ready to accept My Truth.
This is when you experience victory over shortcomings.

Jeremiah 29:11

"For I know the thoughts that I think towards you,
saith the Lord, thoughts of peace, and not evil,
to give you an expected end."

A RENEWED FAITH

There is much I want to say to My people,
yet so many are too busy to stop and listen.
Yes, they want My will and My way for their lives,
but how will they know lest they hear from Me?
I guide My people in many different ways.
To recognize My leading, you must spend time
with Me to learn of My ways.
Spending time, listening.
I love the praises and prayers lifted up to Me.
Do you not think that I would yearn to talk with you?
To have you come into My presence and hear from Me
in your spirit.
Yes, I want to show you many things, that you
might know Me and the power of My
resurrection in your life.
I am restoring those who humble themselves
and pray to new heights.
That they may know and reveal to others,
the wonderful plans I have for them.
Look unto Me, the author and
finisher of your faith.
A renewed faith I bring to all who will listen and
heed to My calling for them.
I am calling My people to pray, expectantly,
and then they will see what I will do
in their midst.

Proverbs 16:3

"Commit thy works unto the Lord, and thy thoughts shall be established."

A SPIRITUAL JOURNEY

Keep focused on Me, your Lord and Savior. See My hand in everything.
Be My example to all those I bring into your life.
Do not interfere with My working in others' lives,
just be there when it is necessary and needed to
bring forth My truth and love to them.
You are the light I have called and set apart
to draw others to new live in Me.
There is a way to reach true fulfillment.
The spirit of those around you hunger, yet they
do not seek to parch their thirst with My Living Water.
To seek Me early while I may be found.
In a quiet place and also gathered together with those of like faith.
There is so much I have to give, yet many will not come to
receive of this free give I offer them.
You are unable to manage this life and the people and
circumstances around you; that is why
My Son's life was sacrificed for you to experience new life in your spirit.
Accepting Jesus Christ by faith and walking in His
will gives you the insight needed to walk through
this spiritual journey I have called you to.
I have made all provision for you, but you must
entrust everything to Me.
For all things are meant to happen with My purpose in mind.
When you see things in My perspective, you know
why I have to watch things happen that grieves Me.
For My people will not truly surrender all.
Continue to "be" all that I need you to be.
Do not try to understand, for the things of God
are beyond understanding.
Walk by faith and keep trusting and knowing that
God is good and worthy to be praised!

1 Peter 4:11

"If any man speak, let him speak as the oracles of God: if any man minister, let him do it as of the ability which God giveth: that God in all things may be glorified through Jesus Christ, to whom be praise and dominion forever and ever. Amen."

A TRUE DISCIPLE

Think about all the people I bring into your life.
Why are they there? I have a special purpose for each one.
Not only for you to give to them; but also for you to receive from them,
You see, I bring My people together for one purpose…
to glorify Me…in the midst of this dying world.
You must bind yourselves together in My love.
This way nothing will move you from following My truth.
No matter what you face in life, My strength will be sufficient to see you through.
Through it all, you will trust in Me and I will bring it to pass.
You will see victory after victory because you choose
to obey Me in all that you do.
Obedience is better than sacrifice, yet true obedience does call for sacrifice at times.
You are set apart, a willing servant, not only to do for others; but to "be" for others.
An example of the believer, a true disciple, disciplined in the things of God.
Accepting the calling of God requires an obedient and submissive
heart, A mind chosen and determined to be stayed on Me and
My purpose and path for each new day.

Psalm 51: 12

"Restore to me the joy of Thy salvation;
and uphold with Thy free Spirit."

A WILLING VESSEL

Here you are, waiting on your God again. This is what
life is all about. Waiting for His divine direction, then walking in it
My hand is on you. As you ask, you shall receive: that I may be glorified in
and through you.
Circumstances come your way so you will seek
Me early, that My will may be done.
There is a way that seems right unto man, yet it leads to destruction.
I have given you a free will and I will let you do as
you so desire…yet if it is not My divine will,
you will suffer consequences.
This journey is a spiritual journey to be walked
by faith; trusting in a living God.
Nothing is impossible with God. Ask and expect,
do I not promise to give you an abundant life?
You can see My hand in all situations.
Now experience My miraculous touch in a very personal way.
Wait and see with great expectation what I have in store for you.
You are My vessel and My Spirit will flow through
you to touch those around you. I am a blessing God.
Reach out and received the blessings
that I have promised those who love Me and
follow Me with their whole heart.

Daniel 12:3

"They that be wise shall shine as the brightness of the firmament;
and they that turn many to righteousness as the stars
forever and ever."

ABUNDANT LIFE

Ah yes, you are blessed because I desire to bless My people.
Why would I not want to?
Yet so many times you have not asked Me to do so.
My hand has been upon you through many
difficult times in your life—yet through them all,
you have experienced the joy of your Lord
as your strength.
Strength to endure, knowing there are always blessings on the
other side of tribulations.
Your faith is renewed and you can soar like
an eagle.
Salvation is only the beginning of new life in Christ.
Now you will experience the abundant life that I promise.
I have brought you through much only to use you
to encourage others in their spiritual walk.
As I have said before many will pass through your
life; and will walk closer to Me because of your influence
on them.
All knowledge and experience you have acquired
is from Me to share and encourage others with.
You will shine forth as never before, as you
go forth in My Name and for My glory.
Let nothing or no one rob you of My plan and
purpose for you.

2 Peter 1:10

"Wherefore the rather, brethren, give all diligence to make your calling and election sure: for if ye do these things, ye shall never fall..."

BE A CHANNEL

Do you realize who gives you your interests and desires? I do.
For I already purposed the things you will accomplish in your lifetime.
That is, as long as you desire to follow Me and my will for you.
Do not doubt or waver in the opportunities I set before you.
I am directing your steps.
Do I not say I will bring out the gifts and calling of God in due time?
All the hidden talents of man are known by the Lord.
I know you better than you know yourself, because I created you.
You really do not know your potential in God.
That is the reason I desire to lead you into all truth.
Even about yourself.
As you yield yourself to Me, I will teach you new things.
You have already done many things that you never thought you'd do.
That is what's so exciting about this spiritual journey.
All that you do for others will return to you twofold.
As you put your trust in God…His way is perfect for you.
Know that My Holy Spirit will teach you all things,
as I desire to flow through you.
You are a channel through which My work can be performed
as planned.
A vessel that allows Me to flow through, and do that which I have
purposed you to do.
You know what I call you to do, and you will do it with a
perfect heart and a willing mind. (1Chroicles 28:9)

Isaiah 55:9

"For as the heavens are higher than the earth,
so are my ways higher than your ways,
and my thoughts than your thoughts."

BE ATTENTIVE

You have only to listen attentively for I long
to speak with you.
The distractions in this world are there to keep
you from Me, and My purpose for you
in this life.
Opposition also, comes at you, because it opposes
My Spirit that is within you.
Remember, those who oppose you and the truth
you speak, opposes Me.
For My light shines forth from you and exposes
the darkness in other's lives.
You have experienced this many times, yet
you fail to recognize when I am using you to
bring others under conviction to My will for them.
You do not need to understand My ways;
just know that circumstances in life are
opportunities for Me to intervene and bring forth fruit.
I have placed certain people in your life
because I know you will not be moved.
You stand firm in what you know is right and
acceptable behavior.
Your quiet spirit is what allows Me to flow out and
touch others in ways you cannot comprehend.
Your obedience to Me and authority will bring
great rewards, but not without a price.
Your faithfulness will always be tried,
your honesty tested.
Stand fast and know I go before in all things.
I will continue to work through you to bring
others closer to Me.

John 12:35

Then Jesus said unto them, "Yet a little while is
the light with you.
Walk while ye have the light, lest darkness come upon you:
for he who walks in darkness knoweth not whither he is goeth."

BE CHILDREN OF LIGHT

It doesn't take much concentration to listen to Me.
Knowing that I desire to speak with you often,
I am always here waiting for you to give me
your undivided attention.
That is all I ask.
It is so easy to become distracted by the
pressures of this world.
Spiritual things seem to take second place in
your day.
Be careful of this. Remember to keep
your mind stayed on Me throughout
your whole day.
Then and only then will you fulfill the
tasks I set before you.
I must be first in your life, then other
things will be in their right perspective.
My walk for you is clear, My path for you is sure.
So many times I tell you,
"This is the way, walk ye in it."
Yet, at times, you walk your own way, and
find yourself suffering the consequences.
Your way will never work.
This is the true test of a follower of Christ.
They walk in My Light and they light
the path for others to learn of Me.
You must desire true obedience to My way,
so I can use you.
Do not question, just obey.
Obedience always brings joy and peace.

2 Timothy 2:15

"Study to show thyself approved unto God,
a workman that needeth not to be ashamed,
rightly dividing the Word of Truth."

BE CHRIST CENTERED

There are so many distractions in the world.
When you really want to hear from Me, your God, you will.
That is why it is so important to be focused on Me continually; even with everything that is going on around you daily, dwell on Me and you will feel my presence.
You will know my voice amidst the many that will try to block Me out.
In your quiet time, there is still life going on around you, yet because you set that time for me, you are more aware that I am there with you.
Realize that I AM is always with you!
There are those who see you and know and feel My Spirit flow through you.
Some will desire what you have in Me,
others will go their own way in spite of your example of the believer set before them.
Do not be affected by other's responses to your determination to serve Me; no matter what the cost.
The calling of discipleship is a calling to a disciplined life...one set apart for and to the things of God.
This world is not your home, you are preparing for a better place.
Center this life I have given you on Me, your Lord and Savior.
I am the author and finisher of your faith.
I am your very breath.
Live and breath in the Holy Spirit's grace and power; and you will see life bloom all around you.
Stay planted in Jesus, Who is your life giver.
You only have one life, live it bringing glory and honor to God.

1 John 5:3

"For this is love for God, that we keep His commandments,
and His commandments are not grievous."

BE COMMITTED

Yes, you are right. People believe and expect that I
am a wishy, washy; you can do anything you want kind of God.
I love you too much to be that way. I care about things
you may do that will only bring you hurt and discouragement.
Read My Word and see the commands I have
for My people, for they are for your good.
You will never understand some of the things I ask of you.
It is not for you to understand or question, just obey.
Trust I have a reason and a purpose for all I ask of you.
My way is a straight and narrow path.
It is a demanding journey, yet it reaps glorious benefits.
When committed, I require much as I test your faith
in regards to yourself and others.
The grief you feel is the grief I feel.
So few of My people know the true sacrifice of
commitment to My way.
This world is a much stronger force on them;
the devil has convinced them his way is better;
yet it leads to their destruction.
They don't want to hear My Truth, they want their own way.
I have not brought you this far to fail, I created you
and I love you with an everlasting love.
Do not waver. Stand firm in the power of the Holy Spirit,
as I lead and use you for My glory.
I have promised to never leave you nor forsake you, and
will use you to bring forth fruit.
Never underestimate the power of obedience and
submission to My will—
especially when only your faith in Me will
enable you to experience true victory.

Philippians 4:11

"Not that I speak in respect of want: for I have learned, in whatsoever state I am, therewith to be content."

BE CONTENT

You have nothing to fear, for you have put your complete trust in Me.
I am in control of all things, I will meet all your needs and even
your desires.
For that is one of My promises to you.
I am the God of Truth—what I say, I will do.
It is man who puts limitations on Me.
Their trust is in their own capabilities because they have not
realized that everything comes from Me.
Be grateful for the life that I have given you.
When you are obedient to Me, I will open the windows
of heaven for you.
You will want for nothing, because when you ask, you receive.
I withhold nothing from My people except when necessary to teach
and direct them back into My will.
You have experienced this at times and wonder, "why no answer".
Yet, in the process of waiting, you have learned that
in all circumstances of life to be content.
Remember…this is the will of God concerning you in Christ Jesus.
See My hand in everyone's life and make them aware
that I desire to work in and through them, as I do you.
I want nothing but the best for them, but they need to allow me to
be the Lord of their lives. I love them and care, but many choose
to walk in darkness, rather than walk in My marvelous light.
Encourage them to follow after Me.
Believe all that I can and will do and then watch Me do it.

Deuteronomy 4:7

"For what nation is there so great, who hath God so nigh unto them, as the Lord our God is in all things that we call upon Him for?"

BE DILIGENT

Commitment—Do you know when you commit to do something,
you have promised yourself, others and Me, your Savior
that you will do it?
Whatever it takes, you will desire to accomplish the task.
True commitment never wavers, but is determined.
This spiritual walk demands commitment in many forms.
You will need to walk by faith, not leaning on your own understanding.
You will walk in the duties set before you and pursue them diligently.
You stand in the gap for those lacking spiritual insight or are
young in their walk with Me; for you do not want them to fall
or fail.
When you commit to time in prayer, remember
it is only through prayer that My plan and purpose for man
can be accomplished.
So whatever you put your mind and hand on to do,
do it heartily as unto the Lord, Your God,
in Jesus' Name,
through the strength and power of the Holy Spirit.
Many of My people are still lost in themselves.
Your spiritual journey is not full of tradition and rituals,
it is an adventure as your spirit submits to My call.
I know what is best for you, listen and heed to my leadings.
Watch and pray; then you will see the salvation of
the Lord; for I am the way, truth and life for all who
come to Me.

Romans 12: 2

"And be ye not conformed to this world: but be ye transformed by the renewing of your mind, that ye may prove what is that good, and acceptable, and perfect, will of God."

BE FAITHFUL

There is no better time than the present to bring your
deepest needs to Me.
At times you're not even sure what some of them are,
nor how they are going to be met.
I am always near to you, and desiring to meet your
every need, yet you don't always bring them to Me.
Draw near to Me so I can show you My will and plan for your life.
When you look to man to fulfill your life, you
will be disappointed. Human nature is selfish.
When you want nothing for yourself, but what
I purpose for you to have, you will see
the windows of heaven open unto you.
In the Word, Jesus says, "Deny Thyself, take up your
cross and follow Me." (Mt 16:24)
Whenever self is on the throne of your life, I am not.
Yield all to Me and trust Me.
Walk in humility, esteeming others more highly
than yourself.
I went about doing My Father's business,
I need you to do the same.
Go, tell others that I love them and
that Jesus saves and transforms lives of those
who are lost and caught in the schemes Satan
deceives them with.
Always remember to come aside, alone, for a time of refreshing and the
renewing of your mind.
Quietly sitting in My presence, drinking in the
solitude and strength of the Holy Spirit refilling you.
For, as you know, the world's deceptions will bring unbiblical and ungodly
ideas into your minds.
Turning you from the Truth to what is false, and leading you astray.
I am all you need to fulfill My purpose for creating you. Seek My will and
way only.
Let others experience My Spirit in you, in all that you say and do.

Matthew 25:21

"His Lord said unto him, Well done,
thou good and faithful servant: thou
has been faithful over a few things,
I will make thee ruler over many things:
enter thou into the joy of thy Lord!"

BE FILLED AND PREPARED

Yes, I always want to speak with you, but
especially when you take your pen in hand to
take note of what I may say to you.
Then I know I have your undivided attention.
This is so necessary at this time of busy
schedules.
I can always speak to your spirit, as you submit
your day to Me, to direct your steps.
What I love most is when your mind is stayed
on Me always.
When in all situations you look to Me for
guidance.
Desire for My Spirit to be in control at all
times, then I will be. I am with you always,
there is never a minute that goes by that I am
not directing your steps as you ask Me to.
My way is not difficult to those who put
their trust in me completely.
All things are working as I have ordained them.
They will always work together for good for
those who love Me.
Walk circumspectly before Me and you will
see Me move among you as never before.
You are realizing My presence more now,
because you are looking for Me and expecting
Me to do what you ask of Me.
I am a faithful God.
Oh, that my people would be faithful to Me,
and trust Me with their very lives.

Matthew 18:3

Jesus said, "verily I say unto you,
except ye be converted, and become as little children,
you shall not enter into the Kingdom of Heaven."

BE HUMBLE

Is something bothering you?
Are you feeling overwhelmed today?
There is nothing to fret or worry about when
you seek to be in My divine will.
There is no struggling when you come in My
perfect will;
the way I have purposed for you from the beginning.
There may be some adjustments you need to make
in your life almost continually.
Without change you will not grow spiritually.
Trust completely in Me when experiencing those changes.
You will see once you follow My way and not
your way of doing things; you will experience
peace, contentment and joy come into your
heart and mind.
Do not fear change, for I do know what is best for you.
I love you.
This is the way, walk ye in it…
by My Spirit says the Lord.

1 Thessalonians 5:16-18

"Rejoice evermore. Pray without ceasing.
In every thing give thanks:
for this is the will of God in Christ Jesus
concerning you."

BE PRAYERFUL

Seek ye first the Kingdom of God and all
things will be added unto you.
Nothing will I withhold from you when it will glorify Me.
When you obey My Word and seek My will,
You will experience the windows of heaven open unto you.
As you are realizing, this walk requires sacrifice,
willingness and availability.
Yet whatever I call you to do is not grievous,
but rewarding.
Oh, at times, it may seem difficult, but you will
have the desire to persevere.
This is because you know it is what I want you to do.
So in everything you do, be prayerful.
For this way you will accomplish the tasks
I set before you.
You will know what your true calling is.
Not everything folk ask of you is My desire for you.
Remember always, that your heart will always
be towards Me in the decisions you have to make.
There is never a doubt when I open the door for you
to walk, for with an open heart you will desire to do it.
A desire so strong that there is no room for doubt.
Choose you this day whom you will serve; and
I will show you the way in which you should go.
I will show you great and mighty things I will
do in and through you for My glory and praise.

Proverbs 16:3

"Commit thy works unto the Lord, and thy thoughts shall be established."

BE REFRESHED

Am I not a God who desires to bless you and meet
all your needs?
Am I not your God who answers your prayers and
directs your path?
Then follow ME, for I desire to move in your life,
so you will see My will unfold for you.
I, alone, know what is best for you.
I bring certain people into your life for My purpose.
By faith you walk the path I have chosen for you.
You need not fear the course your life is taking
right now:
I mean it for good and never to harm you.
You have learned that in this world there are those
who mean to harm you, but I will always
protect you. Yet I do not bring you out
in order for you to turn back.
I have brought folk to you who you can trust.
Lean on them, they love and care about you as I do.
You know who they are, for your heart is telling you.
Go forth into a new refreshing…
receiving the blessings I have prepared for you.
Then you will know and experience My love in a
new dimension.

2 Corinthians 3:17-18

"Now the Lord is that Spirit: and where
the Spirit of the Lord is, there is liberty.
But we all, with open face beholding as in a glass
the glory of the Lord, are changed into the
same image from glory to glory, even
as by the Spirit of the Lord."

BE RENEWED

Looking at the glorious spring weather is a time of refreshing.
This is what it is like when you come into My presence.
Basking in the presence of My Holy Spirit
renews your spirit.
I want your spirit to soar to higher heights and
deeper depths in your walk with Me.
Look to the King of Kings and Lord of Lords for
I am the One who has purpose for your very being.
I know your coming and your going,
your strengths and your weaknesses.
For I am the God who created you. I know
all about you. I care about all the intricate parts
of your life.
This is why I want to direct your steps,
so My will can be fulfilled in and through you.
Come unto Me all ye who are weary, and I will give you rest.
Rest for your very souls.
Come apart from them and drink in My presence.
Then you will be refreshed to carry on the work
I set before you to accomplish.
Time of refreshing awaits you, but you must seek
times of quiet meditation.
Then I will saturate you with the presence and power
of My Holy Spirit.
Drink of the living Water that I freely give until the
recesses of your soul feel satisfied.
This is the only way you can overflow in the Spirit to others.

1 Corinthians 7:7

"For I would that all men were even as I myself.
But every man hath his proper gift of God,
one after this manner, and another after that."

BEING TOO BUSY FOR GOD

You can never be too busy for God, yet many of us
get caught up feeling we have to be a part of everything, and
always on the go.
Come unto Me, and I will give you rest.
Rest for your weary souls. Why do I say this to you; and then say,
do not be weary in well doing?
All My children are given special gifts and callings.
That which I call you to do, is easily accepted, is your hearts desire.
I have already shown you, enter into those things and be diligent.
This allows others to enter the church body with
their God given talents and gifts.
All things I ask of you bring honor and glory unto Me.
I have called all My people to be who I have made them to be.
What you do is important, yet who you are in Christ,
is of the upmost importance.
I need your time and attention to lead and guide you.
Remember always, I do not want you so busy that you have no time
to spend with Me in prayer, in My Word and drawing near to Me.
When you are too busy to nourish yourself in My presence each day,
and learn of Me and My ways…then you will be unable to fulfill
my calling in your life as I so desire.
You will experience frequent set backs and
not understand why. Yet you will realize that
it gets your attention back to Me, as I so want it to be.
BE who I purpose you to BE. DO what I purpose you to DO.
Nothing more, nothing less.
Then you will walk in newness of life, patiently
accomplishing My work on earth together
with the body of Christ, who are My people
called according to My purpose.

Psalm 95: 8, 10+11

"Harden not your heart as in the provocation, and
as in the days of temptation in the wilderness:
Forty years long I grieved with this generation,
it is a people that do err in their heart, and they
have not known My ways: Unto whom I sware in My
wrath that they should not enter into My rest."
Tell the lost Who I AM.

BRING THE LOST TO ME

There are so many voices.
The world is full of people's opinions and thoughts on who I am.
Also the voices of darkness, with the negatives and deception
try to bring confusion to My very elect.
There is only one voice that My people must listen for.
Seek Me with all your heart and you will find Me.
I am never too afar off. Whenever you ask, I will speak
and direct your steps.
Each day when you come to Me, I am waiting to listen.
When you take time with Me, I will come to you and grant
your desires.
I long for an intimate relationship with you.
A closeness that no one can sever.
There is much I have for you to do, as you seek My will each day.
I will open doors of opportunity for you to reach out
and touch the lives of others for My glory.
There is a hungry harvest, lost and dying, without hope.
Think about those I have brought into your life directly.
Be mindful of the calling in Christ Jesus for you to
disciple my People.
Encourage them to learn of Me while there is still time.
The harvest is plentiful, but the laborers are few.
Let nothing hinder you from what I call you to do.
There is nothing so rewarding as serving your Living God;
and bringing others to accept the One True God who
longs to be their Savior and Lord.

Romans 8: 26

"Likewise the Spirit also helpeth our infirmities: for we know not what we should pray for as we ought: but the Spirit itself maketh intercession for us with groanings which cannot be uttered."

BY MY SPIRIT

Being grateful for all the little things I bestow upon you.
This is how My people should be.
It grieves Me to see so many downhearted folk
due to circumstances in their lives.
Wondering where I am and asking why they are
so troubled.
Did I not say, you will have troubles in the flesh?
This is why it is so important to walk and even
think in the Spirit.
My Holy Spirit will help you soar above
the problems in life.
When in pain, the body and mind go to work
to fix it.
Yet, you must realize that true healing comes from God.
Trust Me with everything.
I created your body, I know what it needs.
There are many hurting, and they try to cover it up.
That is not the way to true healing.
Bring your hurts to Me, physical and emotional,
trust Me to guide you, heal you and set you free.
Call on me in prayer that you may experience true
healing in your inner man by the cleansing
power of My Spirit.

Joshua 24: 15b+16

"Choose ye this day whom ye will serve...
God forbid that we should forsake the Lord
to serve other gods."

CHANGES AND CHOICES

Do you remember when you first surrendered your life to Me
to be Savior and Lord over it?
I, your Burden Bearer, lifted you up and set you free.
You knew then that your life was changed, you
were no longer walking after the flesh,
but in the Spirit.
Changes and choices became an intricate part
of your life and still are.
These two words form the guidelines for
the plans I have for you.
When you change your ways and choose
to follow in My designated plan for you;
then you will always experience peace.
If you deter from the path, you will experience uncomfortable
circumstances that are the signs and warnings to
change direction and choose My way.
This is the only way, walk ye in it, I say.
The God of your salvation loves you and desires to
guide your every step.
Will you allow Me to, or would you rather choose
Satan's way or your own way and fail; and
fall short of the glory of God?

John 3:3

Jesus answered and said unto him,
"Verily, verily I say unto thee, Except a man
be born again, he cannot see the kingdom of God."

CHOOSE LIFE

Births—There are so many ways we celebrate them.
New births, birthdays, spiritual births.
Do you know the celebration that goes on in heaven when
one is reborn into God's family?
Our hearts should rejoice whenever someone makes the choice
to come out of bondage to this world into renewed life with Christ.
With any birth, we are celebrating life. True life is in My Son,
Jesus Christ. Ye must be born again.
This is another beginning, allowing your spirit to come alive.
As you accept Jesus, My Holy Spirit comes
to dwell in you, new life is restored.
As you still walk in the flesh, your spirit soares and begins to
desire My will.
Though you are still able to choose your own way at any time,
for life is a choice.
I will draw and teach you by My Spirit to live in right standing with Me.
I chose to give you new life, now I ask to to give it back to me
to nurture and guide to fulfill My purpose for creating you.
Do not look to the left or to the right,
but always look to the author and finisher of your
faith, Jesus Christ.
Strive for the high calling in Christ Jesus which was
prepared for you from the beginning.
Choices are made with your will.
Surrender your will to Me and you will see
Jeremiah 29:11 fulfilled in your life.
I love you with an everlasting, fulfilling love.
I alone give you all you need to sustain life
in a world that chooses sin and death.

Matthew 28:20

"And surely I am with you always, even to the very end of the age."

CHOOSE WISELY

The lack of prayer is the reason the nation has become so corrupt.
My people see wrong being done all around them.
Yet, they do not humble themselves and pray.
This world needs to hear that there is a better way.
Prayer changes things and people.
I tell you, I have a plan and a purpose for every life I have created.
Many choose their own way instead of mine.
There is a way that seems right to man, yet it leads to destruction.
Choose you this day whom you will serve.
The god of this world desires to rob and destroy you.
I have come that you may have life.
My desire for you is freedom from sin and shame;
and an abundant life full of peace and joy.
Surrender all to Me, I long to be Lord and Savior of your life.
Seek My will with all your heart, I know what is best for you.
I will help you through all the difficult trials of life.
For without Me you can do nothing.
With Me all things are possible.
Know that I care for you, more than anyone will ever care for you.
I love you with an everlasting love.
There is no other love like the love of God.

Hebrews 10: 19+22

"Having therefore, brethren boldness to enter into the holiest by the blood of Jesus... Let us draw near with a true heart in full assurance of faith, having our hearts sprinkled from an evil conscience, and our bodies washed with pure water."

CLING TO THE THINGS OF GOD

Notice the still, quiet, almost unnoticed peace that is within your heart.
That is where My Spirit resides and from there you receive life.
You spirit is alive because of My presence within you.
Draw strength each day by coming away to listen to the soft inner voice of My Holy Spirit.
I long to encourage, instruct, guide and admonish my people.
Yet I also yearn to speak with you intimately.
Just you and Me alone in our quiet place.
Your desire towards Me only…listening attentively to all I have to say.
This takes a longing on your part to come away from the busy demands on your life to enter the holy of holies, My presence.
So few try to truly hear from Me.
Some even fear My truth because they do not realize that the truth will always set them free.
For with hearing, also comes the desire to follow.
Encourage others to take time to commune with the God of their salvation.
I will speak with them as well.
My people will know My voice and learn of Me.
Come, I say, draw near to Me and I will draw near to you.

Galatians 5:25

"If we live in the Spirit, let us also walk
in the Spirit."

COME AWAY

Yes, My child, I hear your plea to be a good listener.
As you do with Me, you must do with others…
be attentive to what is being said.
There is much you can learn by listening.
Not only about them, which is very important, but about
yourself as well.
So many need a listening ear and then only a word
of encouragement.
You know who is the Great Counselor, direct
them to Me.
I AM the problem solver, the relationship restorer.
This is a stubborn generation, one seeking
quick fixes.
My people want to hold fast to the things of this world,
rather than the things of God.
My way brings peace, joy, contentment and
confidence that is founded on a firm
foundation.
If Jesus Christ is not the center of all that you do,
then you will fail.
All that is done for My glory and honor will succeed.
All that you do for others, you do unto Me.
Remember that the steps of the righteous are
ordered by the Lord.
All that I call you to do, I will equip you and have
already prepared the way.
When you choose to put Me in the center of your life,
then I AM the center of all that you do.
You will see My will being done all around you
as you pray, read and spread My Word.

2 Thessalonians 1:11

"Wherefore also we pray always for you, that our God
would count you worthy of this
calling and fulfill all the good pleasure of His
goodness, and the work of faith with power."

COME BEFORE ME

There are many voices in the spiritual realm, but
only one Who speaks absolute truth.
Coming before Me often will teach you how
to be sensitive to the voice of the Holy Spirit
from within you.
Your spirit will bear witness to the prompting of the
Holy Spirit, and you will follow My leading.
Just as you write with confidence, as you journal
your thoughts, you will also know what to
say to others.
Listen, as others speak, and I will give the when
and what to say, if anything.
Wait on Me, I say, in every situation.
Remember, you cannot draw others to Me, lest the
Holy Spirit from within is allowed to reach out to them.
Waiting is very difficult, but I must have time to prepare
their hearts to receive what My people have to say.
The flesh must die before the spirit can truly come alive
and be fruitful.
Whoever you are with, pray and seek to be
yielded, that I may flow through you for the work
being done in the lives around you
in My Name and for My glory.
Go forth in My Name and because of your faith,
others will learn and be saved.

Acts 1:8

"But ye shall receive power, after that the Holy Ghost
is come upon your: and ye shall be witnesses
unto Me both in Jerusalem, and in all Judaea,
and in Samaria, and unto the uttermost
parts of the earth"

COME HOLY SPIRIT, I NEED THEE

Have you realized yet that I long for you to experience
My Holy Spirit working in and through you at all times?
As well as in the quiet times you are able to steel
away from a busy day to talk with Me, bring me prayer
needs and maybe even try to listen for My still small voice
speak to you in your spirit.
When difficult situations confront you, I am there
with you, waiting to intercede and show you
what I would have you do.
It seems that you want to take care of everything yourself.
My Spirit dwells in you for a purpose. When you
asked Me to come into your life, I came.
Do you look to Me for everything and in every situation?
I am there to direct and guide each step you take, each problem
that confronts you, and especially every decision
and situation with "others" you may struggle with.
These are the times I want you mindful of My presence
within you and allow My Spirit to be in control.
This means wait, quietly submitting self and the problem or
decision to Me.
I desire to guide you through life's needs always, that I
may be glorified in all that you do.
In all things and at all times TRUST me and
acknowledge Me when you need answers and direction.
For I am the Way, the Truth and the Life,
I, your God, am always with you.
Look for Me and listen. You will hear Me.

1 Chronicles 28:9

"...Know thou the God of thy father, and serve
him with a perfect heart and with a willing mind:
for the Lord searcheth all hearts, and understandeth
all the imaginations of the thoughts: if thou seek Him,
He will be found of thee; but
if thou forsake Him, he will cast thee off forever."

COME UNTO ME

You come to Me in prayer with all the needs
of your loved ones written before you.
I know all that is written and all that is on your heart.
Yet I teach you to come to Me by faith for yourself and others.
I say, "Ask and you shall receive, seek and you
shall find, knock and the door shall be opened unto you."
This is the way you will see My hand in everything
you bring to me each day.
The door of your heart opens to Me in expectation;
knowing I will answer you.
When you seek Me wholeheartedly wanting only My will; then have
confidence that whatever you ask, according to My will,
you will receive.
There is nothing I withhold from My children; yet I require obedience and
devotion to what I call you to do.
Be faithful in reaching out to those I entrust to your care.
You will know them, for they will reach out to you,
because they are still looking for Me.
Oh, they are Mine, they just haven't truly plugged in
to the source to receive all I have for them.
There is so much they miss, when they do not come away
and sit at My feet.
Tapping into the source of their salvation for all their needs.
Enjoy all I give you hear on earth, but always
remember, without Me you would have or be nothing.
In Me—you live and move and have your being.

1 Timothy 4:15,16

"Meditate upon these things; give thyself wholly to them;
that thy profiting may appear to all.
Take heed unto thyself, and unto the doctrine;
continue in them: for in doing this thou shalt both
save thyself, and them that hear thee."

DILIGENCE

When we are diligent in seeking to serve our Lord,
He will show us how to touch those around us
with His transforming power.
Diligence is another virtue I require of My people.
Without it you will not reach your true calling.
By faith you have accepted Me as Lord and Savior
of your life.
Only by faith can you be diligent in desiring
to do all I ask.
Many do things because they think they should
or must.
Diligence in the heart brings forth a strong
desire to accomplish that which I desire
you to do.
Fulfilling My will and encouraging others
I put into your life to do the same.
This will only come by keeping Me on the
throne of your life.
Diligently seeking to know Me and My
resurrection power within you.
For it is through the Power of the Holy Spirit
that all is accomplished for My glory.
Diligently yearn to walk in the Spirit,
yielded to My will and direction.
I have a plan and purpose for you each day.

James 1:25

"But whoso looketh into the perfect law of liberty, and continueth therein, he being not a forgetful hearer, but a doer of the work, this man shall be blessed in his deed."

DO WHAT MY WORD SAYS

Yield your all to Me, the God of your salvation.
I am here with you now.
Longing to tell you the plans I have for you.
Listen, I say, as I speak to your heart.
That is where you will hear My still small voice whisper
to you the mysteries of thy great salvation.
So many times you want to go your own way, and
do your own thing; yet when you yield to ME, you
will follow Me.
In all thy ways acknowledge Me, and I will direct thy path.
Are you walking in the way you should go each and every day?
You can have that confidence as you yield yourself to My Spirit.
I will only come alive in your life when you desire only
My ways and will for your life.
This spiritual walk calls for a yielded, committed people.
Do you desire to be My people?
Well, I desire to be your one and only God.
Come unto me all ye who are heavy labored, and
I will give you rest for your weary souls.
I am your God, only if you so desire, and
I only, love you with an everlasting love.
Christian, do you really know Me
and the power of My Resurrection in your life?

Psalm 16:11

"Thou wilt show me the path of life: In Thy presence is fulness of joy; at Thy right hand there are pleasures forevermore"

Let me show you the way, as you do what My Word says, then showers of blessing will I bring to you.

DON'T QUIT

Do not be weary in doing good, for in the proper time
you will reap a harvest if you do not give up,
Have I not said I will use you as an example to those
around you?
Yes, there have been many difficult situations
I have brought you through in the past.
Only to have you shine for Me.
It is important that you come to Me whenever
the waters of life are troubling you.
This is why you have chosen Me to be your
Lord and Savior.
For My people are a needy people.
This world has a habit of trying to swallow you
up in turmoil.
But, your faith in Me will surely bring you
the answers you need for victory.
I desire to intervene when you ask Me to.
I will remove these circumstances from your life and
once again you will glorify Me with a testimony
of the goodness of your God.
Your life is mine and what I permit to come to you
always has My purpose in mind.
I know how much you can take, and will make a way
of escape for you when things get too much to bear.
For what Father would not intervene for his children.
You are my child and I have come that you
might have life; the abundant life I have promised you.

Hebrews 10:23

"Let us hold fast the profession of our faith
without wavering; for He is
faithful that promised."

DON'T STRUGGLE—YIELD

I am using you when you do not even know it.
Your life, surrendered to Me, is a beacon for all to see.
Even when you falter, those around you know whom you lean on.
They know you trust Me with you whole being.
I have made you and formed you in My image.
Will I not guide your every step, meet your every need?
I long to bless My people.
Yet, you do not ask for those things you think are impossible.
Because in you human mind and effort, they are.
I am your God and with Me ALL things are possible.
For when you ask according to My will, you will receive.
I am a miracle working God, why must I wait for My people
to ask of Me, so I may be glorified in all I do for them.
Ask, wait and see how I move in the midst of those
who fully rely on Me.
I desire to be an intricate part of your every day activities.
So intricate that you see My every intervention in all
that you do.
You desire to spend time with Me, more intimate, quiet
time, so you can experience My presence.
Draw close, I am here.

Psalm 37:5

"Commit thy way unto the Lord;
trust also in Him; and He shall bring it to pass."

DRAW CLOSE, I AM HERE

I want you to know and be aware of My Presence.
I desire to have a part in every situation that confronts you.
Come before Me silently when you do not know what
to do or say.
Submit it to Me immediately before opening your mouth.
Then and only then will My purpose be done in any situation.
When you put me in control, I can use you to bring forth
my will.
Otherwise I must use other means to bring the changes
I require of you.
Change is good and you must be willing to make
necessary changes throughout your life.
Seek and desire only what I want for you.
When you go your own way and do your own thing,
I must deal with it; work out that which is not pleasing to Me.
When you are in My divine will there is peace and joy.
There is no struggle.
You struggle when you want your own way, and I am
not allowing it.
Surrender all to Me. Speak with Me often; more than with others.
I am your Burden Bearer
I alone bring release and carry you through difficulties in life.
Only if you allow Me to.

1 Thessalonians 4:18; 5:11

"Therefore encourage each other with these Words."
"Wherefore comfort yourselves together,
edify one another, even as also ye do"

ENCOURAGE OTHERS

Do you realize how special you are to Me?
My people who will humble themselves and pray and
seek My will in all they do, will be used
tremendously to bring glory to My Name.
Seeking not their own way or will, but
desiring always to follow Me.
You are a true disciple when you subject yourself
to the task of encouraging others to learn of Me.
Isn't it sad that My people whom I created
do not believe that I desire to take care of them.
They wish to go their own way…to and fro…
without any direction or purpose.
Generation after generation struggles with problem
after problem. They do not put the God of their salvation
on the throne of their lives.
Then and only then can I fulfill the true purpose of their being.
Believe that the God of all creation desires for you to
know him and His resurrection power.
My ways are not your ways. My way brings life,
not death; peace not strife; joy not depression.
Those who follow Me will not struggle nor strive;
but will rest and walk in the calling I have for them.
A victorious place!
To win the lost at any cost. I will show you the way
For I AM the way, WALK YE IN IT.

James 5:11

"Behold, we count them happy which endure.
Ye have heard of the patience of Job,
and have seen the end of the Lord;
that the Lord is very pitiful, and of tender mercy."

ENDURE TO THE END

There will always be circumstances and people that
will be very difficult to contend with in this world.
This is when you must endure and persevere through faith.
Knowing I will bring you through to victory.
I place people in your life at different times for different
reasons and purposes.
You are together for one main purpose and that
is to bring glory to My Name.
Others in your life may work against you and my purpose.
You must take a stand, endure them and still love them.
This does not mean allow them to negatively affect
your spiritual walk in any way.
Your walk needs to affect them in a positive way.
It should and will bring their focus to Me.
At times just your presence will bring conviction,
because I flow through you and My light shines on the
darkness in their lives.
This can make folk most miserable, for darkness
hates the light.
Pray for them diligently and speak truth to them that
My truth can set them free.

John 3:16

"For God so loved the world, that He gave His only begotten Son, that whosoever believeth in Him should not perish, but have everlasting life."

EVERLASTING LOVE

Do you know how precious you are to me, your Lord?
You are a child of God and I love you.
So many times you wonder what I am going to have
you do next, fearful of your ability.
Yet, when you step out in faith and obey my leading,
I am able to bless you abundantly.
You are learning that whatever I ask of you is not difficult,
even when a challenge, you come out the victor.
I, your God, give you testimony as to the wonderful
works I perform in your life, that you may bring glory to the
God of your Salvation.
This is what your life is all about…walking in the newness
of the life I have given you through My Son, Jesus Christ.
When you follow Me in all that you do, blessings follow you.
You become a light for the world to see
and know that I am the living God,
who desires to give them life.
A life that glorifies Me, the God and Father
of those who truly commit to Me; and
obey and follow what I ask them to do.
Show forth My light to this dying world that I
once again may be King of Kings and Lord of Lords
in this lost generation of vipers.
What is happening around you now is not My plan.
You know I created man to glorify Me.
Go forth in obedience, listen and heed to My
calling to save the lost at any cost.
You will then see the blessings of your salvation
come to pass.
Go, I say, and tell them that I, their God loves them.

Proverbs 16:9

"A man's heart diviseth his way: but the Lord directeth his steps."

FAITH AND DETERMINATION

Do you know how important you are to Me,
the God who created you?
You hold the keys to My kingdom in
your hands.
Only through My people can My Word spread
throughout the world.
Yield to Me, follow Me and I will tell
you what to say.
Let others see Me in you and hear My voice
as I speak through you.
Pray, they may desire My power in their lives also.
All I need is a vessel of honor that I
may use and flow through.
You are that living vessel, walk in that calling
by faith and determination.
I am with you today as always. You are very special.
I care about your every day tasks and go
before you as you accomplish them.
Are you aware of My presence?
Know that I protect you and care about even the
smallest details of your day.
Care about one another, as I care for you.
Let My love flow through you to those who are lost.
Only through My people can I show them the way
to my saving grace and so great a salvation.

Isaiah 30:15

"For thus saith the Lord God, the Holy One of Israel; In returning and rest shall ye be saved; in quietness and confidence shall be your strength..."

FAITH AND EXPECTATION

Be not concerned about the length of time you spend
in quiet devotion with Me;
but the quality of time you spend in My presence.
Yes, you will learn of me through My Word.
I will speak with you there; and also as you go about
your daily tasks.
What I long for is when you do sit before Me quietly;
awaiting to commune with Me.
This is when your faith will truly soar, and
you will receive personal instruction, direction,
correction and true guidance from the
Holy Spirit within you.
You see, you must exercise true faith to know
My voice. Come before Me with great
expectation, giving me the opportunity to
speak with you, and I will.
Do whatever it takes that makes you attentive to Me.
With some it may be to take up your pen;
Knowing, expecting and waiting to hear from God.
This is submission, openness and humbleness.
For you have realized that in Me you live and
move and have your being.
Hearing from Me continually gives you strength
to carry on; wisdom and faith to be My
disciple; and the boldness to witness of
the true value and cost of this life in Christ.
There is no other way.
Put your trust in Me and be thou My example
to those around you.

Colossians 3:16

"Let the Word of Christ dwell in you richly in all wisdom."

FEED YOUR SPIRIT

An end to something, is always a beginning of something new.
New opportunities and challenges in this corrupt world.
Daily appointments and decisions to be made continually.
Oh, how much easier life is when you choose
to allow God to instruct and direct you.
You see, everything is your choice, for I have
given you a free will.
You even choose how much you desire to feed your spirit.
However, most of My people are starving themselves
in this area.
Thinking and believing it is more important to feed their
bodies and minds.
BALANCE, my people, is so necessary as you take this
journey with Me.
You can never do too much with Me and for Me,
because I am the only way to true life.
I am life, without me you can do nothing.
You must walk and talk and even breath Jesus, for this
is how to walk in the Spirit.
The very breath you breath is the breath of God.
What you feed into your mind, body and spirit will show
forth in your every day activities.
You choose continually to follow the ways of the world,
your own ways, or God's way.
Choose ye this day to follow after righteousness. (right living)
A life pleasing in God's sight.
Rightly dividing the Word of God and applying it
to your life as a daily diet is to know Me and the
power of My resurrection flowing through you.

Isaiah 12:2

"Behold, God is my salvation; I will trust, and
not be afraid: for the Lord JEHOVAH is
my strength and my song;
He is also is become my salvation."

FOCUS ON JESUS

This ought not to be, It is too easy to get caught
up in the things of this world and not give Me
the time you need.
You have come too far to turn back now.
Listen to Me and obey.
This is the time for perseverance in whatever
I call you to do.
Be my example, be faithful.
Be careful not to follow any man, especially
just to please him,
you are to follow only ME, as I lead and guide
your steps.
Do not question, walk where I take you and
show forth My love and Light
to those lost in grips of this dark world.
"Be not afraid, only believe."
I, your God, has a purpose for all of you being here.
Let Me show you.
One day at a time.

Proverbs 4:13

"Take fast hold of instruction; let her not go:
keep her; for she is thy life."

FOLLOW ONLY ME

In your busy life, it is so very important to be ever mindful
of my presence.
I love it when you speak to Me about the events of your day.
And when you turn to Me for help and direction.
You see, I am always there for you.
There is nothing to big for your God.
I am a blessing God, yet many do not look for my blessings,
nor even expect them.
So they do not see them or recognize when they do come,
that they are from Me.
Many of my people are focused on their shortcomings,
limitations and problems.
I want you focused on Me, the author and finisher of your faith.
I, alone, give you strength
to accomplish the things I call you to do.
Continue on in faith, and see what I will bring to pass
in your life.
I know what is best for you, and I also know what will keep
you close to Me.
If you ignore Me, you will go your own way and fail.
but when you focus on Me you will
discover this spiritual journey I have you on.
A journey that is everlasting, and brings victory
to the steps you take.
Come to Me and I will give you true rest
in the Holy Spirit; Who abides in you, and
brings you comfort.
Focus and Trust and you will see
wisdom from heaven come to thee.

Psalm 29: 1+2

"Give unto the Lord, glory and strength.
Give to the Lord the glory due unto His Name.
Worship the Lord in the beauty of holiness."

FOR MY GLORY

There is much going on around you.
I am so glad when you see My hand in everything you see.
I allow everything in order to show My people
My will and way for them.
Nothing else works unless you follow after righteousness.
Even righteous living has to come from Me.
I made you and I desire to transform you into My image.
As you surrender more and more of yourself, and the things
of this world to Me; you will experience My will and
purpose for your life.
All that you do is to be for My glory.
If it is going to glorify Me, then by all means pursue it.
Your steps I have already ordered, but you must choose
to follow the path I have ordained for you each day.
I promise to guide you into all truth.
The life I give you permeates truth through
your whole being.
The Holy Spirit's indwelling presence cleanses you
from all unrighteousness; and enables you to walk
honestly and uprightly before others.
You must realize there are many who will not hear
you, because of their stubborn hearts.
As My disciple you must speak the truth in spite of
reactions and rejections, for in time the truth will set them free.
Obedience is not always comfortable, but always
reaps rewards. In my Kingdom there is nothing so
necessary as obedience to the prompting of My Holy Spirit
within the believer.
Go forth in My Name and in the strength and power of my anointing.

Matthew 5:16

"Let your light so shine before men that they may see your good works, and glorify your Father which is in heaven."

FULFILL MY COMMISSION

Do you know that all that you do is
ordained by Me?
Even when the waters around you are troubled,
think not that I won't use you.
A disciplined life is one who has put Me and
the things of God first and foremost in their life.
Nothing else matters, but what I would have you do.
When you are submitted to Me, everything
you do and say has a purpose.
To fulfill the great commission.
To reach out and touch the lost. This means
those who have found My great salvation
want to tell others about this wonderful
life changing experience.
Study and pray that you may have the
words to speak.
You can only do this with singleness of mind
and heart.
Hungering and thirsting after righteousness.
Then you will be filled and used of God
to show for His light in this world full
of darkness.

Psalm 100:4

"Enter into His gates with thanksgiving, and into his courts with praise: be thankful unto Him and bless His Name."

GIVING THANKS

Celebrating together all your God has bestowed upon you.
Look around you and absorb just who your God is to you.
No matter what age you are, if you know me
as your Savior, then you have much to be thankful for.
Though troubles may encumber you, even at this time,
I am here to bring you comfort and joy.
As I remind you of the things, times and people
that have brought you peace and pleasure for
as long as they have been a part of your life, and still may be.
Grateful hearts are those who know that
I am with them always, they are never alone; for
I have placed the right people in your life,
that I may meet your needs through them.
Yes, rejoice over the God of your Salvation
in grateful admiration for Who I AM, your Lord and Savior.
Be thankful for everything and everyone.
My will being done on earth.
May not seem that way at times, yet all things are working,
for I am the God of this world and My love is
everlasting and I give you a world without end.
GIVE THANKS
Is it really possible to give thanks in all circumstances?
Yes, we are to cultivate a thankful spirit—giving thanks
for the good things in life, and looking for ways in which
God brings blessings out of even the most difficult experience.

Matthew 22:37

"Jesus said unto him, thou shall love the Lord thy God with all thy heart, and with a thy soul and with all thy mind."

GLORIFY ME

Oh how the thoughts and intents of the heart must be
guarded at all times.
Examine your thought patterns often.
I have purpose for your life.
You must be so intent on fulfilling that purpose that
there is no time to be effected by what others do or say.
Look for Me, seeing Me in all circumstances of life.
Looking at everything in My perspective can only be possible
through the work of My Holy Spirit in you.
The things of this world, the flesh and Satan are all at
work to entrap you.
They work together constantly to try to keep you ineffective
in the calling I have for your life.
Be mindful that who and what you surrender your mind,
time and life, you become servants to.
Choose you this day who you will serve.
I have called you out of bondage into the liberty of My Spirit
who dwells in you.
You, alone choose to turn back into the yolk of bondage.
Do not turn back. Do not even think the thoughts of the past,
except to glorify Me and edify the body of Christ.
Even your very thoughts can put enmity between
you and Me, and you and the brethren.
Concentrate on the things of God and you will renew
the attitude of your mind. and glorify Me in all you do and say.

1 Peter 3:15

"But sanctify the Lord God in your hearts:
and be ready always to give an answer to every man
that asks you a reason of the hope
that is in you with meekness and fear."

GO IN MY NAME

You have been brought through many trials to only increase
your faith in God, your Father.
Have I not cared for you as I care
for the birds in the air?
The birds come to your yard and do they
not expect to be fed?
I gave my life that you may have life.
Life on earth is a constant commitment to tarry until I come.
My covenant is to provide all your needs.
Waiting is a training in faith and endurance.
I will answer when you ask…in My way and
in My time.
Other's trials are for their perfection,
their spiritual healing, for only I know what
brings focus to Myself.
I have given My life that those who will
follow My will for their lives will have
an abundant life.
Trust and obey, for there's no other way to be happy
in Jesus, than to trust and obey.
Decide today to surrender all to your Mighty God;
that I may truly be Lord of your life.
I desire to do great things in the midst of My people.
My power and anointing will be upon them
to go forth in My name.
to call the lost back into my fold.
Go in My name and because you believe,
others will know and be saved.

Hebrews 10:35+36

"Cast not away therefore your confidence, which has great recompense of reward.
For ye have need of patience, that, after ye have done the will of God, ye might receive the promise."

GO IN PEACE

A new year brings new beginnings.
Watch with expectation
for all I have in store for you in the
months ahead.
I long to give you the desires of your heart;
for I have put those desires there.
I want mostly to set you free from the
worldly pressures that oppress you.
I am able to deliver you as you will see.
I have always used you in ways you were not even
aware of. I still do.
You are My vessel. Your life shines My light
into the darkness of this world.
Your faith is being renewed and strengthened.
Be encouraged; trust in Me for I will bring you the victory!
There is nothing too difficult for Me, the God of your Salvation.
Yes your life's journey can be an exciting adventure
when you draw near to Me and know you are Mine,
and I am your God.
You are the servant of the Most High God.
Your life will touch many lives as you walk
the walk I have planned for you.
God in peace and know.
I am with you always.

Ezekiel 36:26+28

"A new heart also will I give you, and a new Spirit
will I put within you: and I will take away the
stony heart out of your flesh, and I will give you
an heart of flesh…
And ye shall dwell in the land that I gave
to your fathers; and ye shall be my people,
and I will be your God."

GO WHERE I SEND YOU

Do you want a new beginning? Be willing to venture out by faith.
The world is a harvest field. I have called you to be My light in
this world of people lost in darkness.
I am the light of this world, and those who choose to follow Me
desire to go where I send them and share their
God given talents with others.
Everywhere, there are opportunities to tell them
about Salvation through Jesus Christ.
More than ever before it is necessary for you
to do what I have called you to do.
Trust me, and know that I will never lead you astray.
There is a reason for everything, though you may not know it.
Question not, but continue the path that I have made just for you.
You and I are on that path together. Every step you take is
ordained by Me, when you put your faith in Me.
That is why you can feel confident that
I will make it evident what you are to do.
I leave no doubts that I am leading you; for when
you choose to walk with Me, I receive the glory for being
an intricate part of your life; as I so very much desire to be.
Only as you ask Me, can I answer you and fulfill the
desires of you heart.
Wait and watch as I do this for you.

John 7:38

"He that believes on Me, as the Scripture
hath said, out of his belly shall flow
rivers of living water."

GOD HEARS US

I am your God, you are my child; and
you are under My care.
Walk in the way I shall lead you.
Many shall pass through your life, and will learn
from your godly example.
Come unto Me often and receive My promised rest.
Sitting quietly before Me in My presence, and
drinking in the living water that comes to you
by My Holy Spirit.
Soon you will experience, once again My power
to bring forth those petitions that are bearing
on your heart.
Have I not promised to meet all your needs?
Haven't I done so thus far?
Then trust Me to bring forth that which
seems impossible to you.
I am able to do all things well, that
you ask of Me.
Watch and see how I bring it all to pass in
My time.
You are under My care and I have promised
to always answer your hearts cry unto Me.
Remember there is a time and a season
for Me to bring forth the fruit of
your labor.
Trust in Me.

1 Chronicles 28:9

"...Know the God of thy father, and serve
Him with a perfect heart and a willing mind:
for the Lord searches all hearts, and understands
all the imaginations of the thoughts:
if thou seek Him, He will be found of thee;
but if thou forsake Him, He will
cast thee off forever."

GOD LOVES YOU

It is always so nice when you take time away from your
busy schedule to spend quiet time with God, knowing
I desire to speak to you.
Never will I let My people down when they
want to hear from Me.
You have experienced many changes in this road of life.
Many roadblocks also, but as you ponder over life's
trials, you see My hand guiding you.
You long to settle down now and rest; yet you also long
to serve Me. Can you not do both?
Being My disciple does not mean always being busy.
I have told you that I use your life as a light
for others to see all that is possible for
someone totally surrendered to Me.
Enjoy, I say, this new dimension of life I am
bringing you into.
Enjoy all the people I have placed in your life,
they are there to bless you, and for you to bless them.
Receive from Me the abundant life so many
long for, but never reach for.
This life will always ask for some sacrifice on your part,
but in the end reaps blessings and rewards.
Remember, I sacrificed My life for you
that you might be a vessel of honor for Me;
to go forth in My name and touch other's lives.
Tell them I love them with an everlasting love.

Isaiah 49:6

"I will also give thee for a light to the Gentiles, that
thou may bring my salvation unto the
end of the earth."

GOD NEEDS YOU

I am your Lord and I love you with
an everlasting, unconditional love.
I long to walk with you and have
conversations with you.
There is never a time when I am not
watching over you.
I even send My angels to help and protect you.
You think of Me as a God that would be in need
of nothing.
Ah, but I need you.
I have kept My people on earth to use them,
flow through them, and light the world
with My Truth that they may be set free, as you
have been.
I will touch lives through those who are
attentive and obedient to Me, their Lord and
Savior.
When you submit yourself to My will, I will give
you power from on High.
As I direct, you will know what to do, what
to say and when to say it.
Seek Me early, while I may be found.
I have promised to show you the way.
Trust with all your heart, desire only
what I would have you do and have.
You will see the windows of heaven
open unto you to meet your every need.

1 Timothy 6:12

"Fight the good fight of faith, lay hold on eternal life, where unto thou art also called, and hast professed a good profession before many witnesses."

GOD PROVIDES

So many obstacles in this life. So many curves in the road.
You must know that you are on the straight and narrow
path, when you recognize My constant guidance.
I am your provider, am I not?
Have I ever let you down?
Whenever you turn to Me, I am there to
meet your every request.
I am leading you to a haven of rest to use
you as I have equipped you for my service.
You have experienced working around the enemy's
camp; and fought the good fight many times.
I made the way for you to escape again and again.
Have you seen My hand in all of this?
You have chosen My will for you life.
Because of this, I have chosen to bless you, and
make you a blessing to others.
Go forth into the harvest field of those who
long to hear about Me.
I will bring much fruit into your life
to nurture.
Encourage them to read My Word and learn of Me;
to grow in faith and in the
knowledge of Jesus Christ their Lord.

Colossians 1:11

"Strengthened with all might, according to His glorious power, unto all patience and long suffering with joyfulness."

GOD'S KEEPING POWER

So often My people look everywhere for the
answers to the simplest things in life.
I AM the answer to everything.
Look to Me, the Author and Finisher of your faith.
there is not a time that I would not be there for you.
Call on Me and I will answer.
times will come when you need direction—
wait on Me and I will show you the way.
The only right answer to everything in this life
is what I would have you do.
Seek first the Kingdom of God and all
these things will be added to you.
When you are about My business,
I will make provision for your needs.
You will experience whatever you put your heart
and mind in prayer to do, I will
bring it to pass by My way and will for you.
I am in the midst of all you endeavor to do,
in My Name and for My glory; for I have
ordained it from the beginning.
Have confidence that I go before you and prepare the way.
There is nothing too difficult when you put all your
trust in Me.
I will never let you down.
You will let yourself down whenever you do not
obey the prompting of My Holy Spirit within you.
Speaking to you from the recessing of your soul.
Be responsive to My voice, and you will follow
after Me; and I will keep you in the path
I have purposed for you.

2 Samuel 22:31

"As for God, His way is perfect; the Word of the Lord is tried: He is a shield to all who trust in Him."

GOD'S SPIRIT IS WITHIN YOU

Do you realize that all thoughts that are towards Me, glorify Me?
I would have you to know this.
I give you interests and desires, yet you must use self control
in all areas of life.
For only then will there be a balance.
I say moderation in all things.
This will always keep things in right perspective.
If you question a decision, do not move without experiencing
that peace that only I can give you.
All that I do and all that I say brings peace, never confusion or discord.
That is the work of the adversary. I want only good for your life.
As I bring people into your life, I will touch their lives through you.
Be the example I have called you to be,
bearing a Jesus likeness and a genuine love for others.
As for your needs and desires, be content in the state
your are in, watch and wait to see My hand move once again
in your life to bring fulfillment.
Be aware of the things you do in secret, does it glorify Me?
If not, STOP now, that you not allow evil to
destroy you and your Christian testimony.
Remember always that our human nature starves
to satisfy the flesh. This ought not to be.
Seek my ways only and you will walk the path I have
purposed for you.
Your life is not your own, you were bought with a price, You are Mine.
I am your God and desire to use you in ways
you are not aware of.
Yet I cannot use a vessel who will bring shame to My Name
by any hidden things you do. Be mindful of this.
Walk, I say, in truth as My Spirit directs your steps.

Proverbs 8: 32+33

"Now therefore hearken unto Me, O ye children:
for blessed are they that keep My ways.
Hear the instruction, and be wise,
and refuse it not."

GOD'S WAY

Put on the full armor of God
so that you can fight against the devil's evil tricks.
Our fight is not against people on earth,
but against the rulers and
authorities and powers of this world's darkness,
against the spiritual power of evil in the heavenly world.
Keep alert and pray.
Let all the godly confess their rebellion to the Lord
while there is time, that they may not drown in the
flood waters of judgment. The Lord says,
"I will guide you along the best
pathway for your life. I will advise you and watch over you.
Many sorrows come to the wicked,
but unfailing love surround those
who trust the Lord." Rejoice in the Lord and be glad, all you who obey Him.
NO HILL IS TOO HIGH,
NO MOUNTAIN TOO TALL,
FOR WITH FAITH IN THE LORD
YOU CAN CONQUER THEM ALL.

Psalm 139:10

"Even there shall thy hand lead me, and thy right hand shall hold me."

GROW IN GRACE

For everything there is a purpose.
As I lead you each day, be confident.
Whatever you put your hands to, you will
accomplish, when you desire My will.
Will I not want to keep you there?
Being with you to assure you fulfill the
calling of God given you.
For My way is not burdensome, but exciting;
when you truly choose to walk with Me.
What I call you to do, will be a delight for
you to do.
Go forth by faith and you will see My hand in
all that you endeavor to do.
I look after My people who seek
their personal spiritual journey.
I am a blessing God, yet remember this,
the more that you have been given,
the more is required of thee.
As you learn of Me, tell the world.
Whatever abilities and talents given you,
share with others that they may feel My
presence through you.
Most importantly walk close to Me and listen
when you are quiet.
Those are the times I long for most.
Then I know you care enough to spend time
out of your busy day to come aside and
hear what I have to say.

2 Peter 3:18

"But grow in grace, and in the knowledge of our
Lord and Saviour Jesus Christ.
To Him be glory both now and for ever. Amen."

HAVE CONFIDENCE

Do you see my hand on your life?
Every corner you turn, every bump in the road
of your journey; I am there to direct you and
smooth the way.
Remember, I have a plan for you.
You have a destiny to fulfill.
Long only to glorify Me and that you will do.
Though you may seem to struggle and even stumble;
I will lift you up and bring you through.
As your faith in Me strengthens
through every difficulty; I will shine more and
more in your life.
Those around you will know that I am your God.
Spend time with Me. I miss you when you do not sit in
my presence.
Allowing my Spirit to overshadow you and
empower you to go forth in My Name.
Do not weary in well doing.
I am watching out for you.
I promise to meet all your needs,
even those you are not even aware you have.
Put all your faith and trust in Me and see the
salvation of your God come to pass
in many more
lives that pass your way.

Joshua 1:9

"Have not I commanded thee? Be strong
and of a good courage; be not afraid,
neither be dismayed:
for the Lord thy God is with thee
wherever you go."

HEAVENBOUND PRIORITIES

Receive My refreshing touch this day. As your latest
journey has been a rugged one.
A journey of mixed emotions. You realize that wherever
you go and whoever you are with, My work goes on.
It continues wherever I send you.
You are My disciple, do you not see the importance of
a disciplined life?
People are always watching how a Christian lives.
How they conduct their daily happenings; and what
takes predominance is what really matters.
The things of God must matter most.
Oh, how the things of this world take precedence even
in the life of a believer.
Why do you suppose that is?
How they love to cater to their flesh, yet
it is their spirits that are hungry.
Nothing else really satisfies, only but
for a brief time.
What is done for Christ last through eternity.
Know this, that much of your testimony for Me will
be left with your family.
Though you feel you didn't say much, your
unspoken words did much.
A mission was accomplished, a good work was done.
There is never a time that I don't send you, but for My
will and purpose to be accomplished in and through you.
As a result you will see the fruit of your labor,
as your living testimony touches others lives.

Romans 8:6

"For to be carnally minded is death; but
to be spiritually minded is life and peace."

HEAVENLY REWARD

There is a way that seems right to man, yet
it leads to destruction.
When I say do not look to the left or to the right,
this means your focus must be on Me.
First and foremost in your day's appointments,
ask, what is your will for me today, Lord?
Be willing to go when asked to go.
Everything you do for others, your do unto Me.
When you seek to do for others, you
are putting yourself aside.
This is the sign of true discipleship.
Disciplined to go and do when called on.
When others do not want to hear and heed
to the call of God for their lives; be there to
encourage them, being careful not to fall
into their lifestyle.
There is a hungry harvest out there—reach out
and touch those who desire to walk the walk
God has purposed for them
Encourage their focus on the things of God,
rather than the things this world has to offer them.
The world and the devil is trying to rob them of all
I have to give them. Yet it is of their own choosing.
For I ask My people to forsake all and follow Me;
working toward their heavenly reward,
not for earthly gain.
If you don't need it or use it for My glory, you don't
need it at all, for I have not ordained for you to have
those things.

Romans 8:28

"And we know that all things work together for good to them that love God, to them who are the called according to His purpose."

HIS CALLING

Do you know those times
when you don't feel that I am close to you,
or yourself close to Me?
It is when I am the closest, watching over you.
Many times I try to get your attention.
Longing for you to experience how real
your relationship with Me can be.
Be open with me and share with me
your innermost thoughts.
I listen and answer the cries
of My people.
Trust the guidance of My Holy Spirit
within you.
Look to Me, only, for answers and guidance.
Go forth in complete confidence
knowing I am in control,
as you allow Me to be so.

Psalm 89:15

"Blessed is the people that know the joyful sound:
they shall walk, O Lord, in the light
of Thy countenance."

HIS PRESENCE

It is so good to take time to be quiet in My presence.
A difficult thing to do in this present age
with so very much to be done!
Minds are always filled with the things of this world.
How can I speak and direct your path
lest you desire to come before Me to receive My plan for you?
Remember, I am a patient and loving God.
the world i moving so quickly, but you can slow down.
Take things as I bring them to you and enjoy.
Be not in a hurry to make things happen.
I have placed others in your life to help you.
You will know that I have blessed you with
certain faithful friends, chosen to bless your life.
Be attentive, for I will use them and speak
through them to help you on your journey.
More folk will come, some for you to minister to,
and some to minister to you. You are on a spiritual journey.
This life is only temporary.
When you desire My will for your life with your
whole heart, I will give you all you need
to fulfill My purpose.
That includes being with the right people at the right times.
Walk in faith and be My example in this dark world.
Shine My light that others may see and learn of Me
through you; till I call you home.

James 4:10

“Humble yourselves in the sight of the Lord,
and he shall lift you up.”

HUMBLE THYSELF

Always be ready, even when you think
you are unsettled
For you do not know the plans I have for you.
Yes, I desire to give you the desires of your heart.
I long to bless you; as you have given
of yourself to others,
I will give back to you twofold.
Look to me and expect to see My hand move
in miraculous ways in your life.
As you have seem many times already,
this too shall pass.
You wonder why you do some things, then
you see my purpose for it as time passes.
Yes, I am guiding your steps, be confident that
you will not stumble.
I desire to bless you, and it is right and good that
you ask Me to do so.
I am the One who stirs your heart to move
forward and make changes in your life.
This is the way, walk ye in it; and receive
the blessings of your Lord.

2 Chronicles 20:15

"And he said, Hearken ye, all Judah, and ye inhabitants
of Jerusalem, and thou king Jehoshaphat, Thus saith the Lord
unto you, Be not afraid nor dismayed by reason of
this great multitude;
for the battle is not yours, but God's."

I AM YOUR GOD

There is nothing I wouldn't give you. There is a price
when doing things your own way.
When choosing My will and way for your life, know that
your flesh and your spirit will always wage war
with each other.
Ah, but My Spirit now dwells within you, and
will always seek victory for you.
Do I not promise to meet all your needs?
Wait and see the blessings I will bestow upon you
for your obedience and strong desire to please
Me instead of man or self.
I have not allowed anything in your live by chance.
My purpose will be done and fulfilled when
you so desire it.
Be open to My guiding hand, and you
will experience much joy.
More than you've ever felt before.
Just know that even in this I am a part.
Working a perfect work in you, so you will have no doubts.
Wait, I say, on your Lord, and
you will see what I can do for and with you.
Leave all in My hands and I will
work ALL things together for your good.
For you love Me and can know
that yo u are called according to My purpose.
I do want the best for you, for I am your Lord and Savior.

1 Corinthians 11:1+2

Paul says, "Be ye followers of me, even as I also
am of Christ. "Now I praise you, Brethren
that ye remember me in all things,
and keep the ordinances, as I delivered them to you."

I WILL SHOW YOU

Be anxious for nothing and with all prayer
and supplication bring your requests to Me.
Then you must wait for the answer.
I will give you direction in your walk.
My timing is always carefully chosen.
As doors of opportunity open, walk through them.
Do not question the motivation in your heart that
moves you forward to seek the unknown.
Mine is a journey of the unknown,
a journey of faith.
This is how I am glorified on the earth.
Those of old stepped out in faith, trusting me
with their very lives; and saw all come to pass
as I said it would.
You can accomplish anything when you put your trust
in Me, pursue even that which seems impossible.
You will see that I am able to guide you where
you have never been before; and show
you how to do things you have never done before.
Follow Me, yes I am guiding you.
Do not wonder when or how; I will teach you.
Go where I lead and do as instructed to do.
I promise to go before you and prepare
the way and make it clear for you.
Availability and willingness always brings
good fruit and glorifies Me.

Romans 15:13

"Now the God of hope fill you with all joy and peace in believing, that ye may abound in hope, through the power of the Holy Ghost"

JOY TO THE WORLD

The Lord has come!
What does that mean to you?
Have you experience the wonderful
joy of knowing the Lord and Savior of your soul?
The One who died for you to set you free,
and desires to fill you with joy unspeakable
and full of glory. Yes, you!
Joy is not just being happy, joy is having the inner feeling
that all is well, because we have received
life in God's Son, Jesus Christ.
Born to die, that we might have everlasting life.
He, alone, gives joy…the things
of this world are temporary,
the things of God are everlasting.
We are at home with Him only when
we know in our hearts He has forgiven us
and saved us from sin and death.
All is well, come unto Me all ye who are lost,
The joy of the Lord is your strength to get through
in a world filled with sin and shame.
Do not look to the left or to the right…
look up to the heavens so you can draw near to Me.
Accept My free gift of Salvation, so
you can receive the joy that lifts you above
all life's burdens and lights the path of hope
I have prepared for you from the beginning.

Acts 6:4

"But we will give ourselves continually to prayer,
and to the ministry of the word."

KEEP ALERT AND PRAY

Put on the full armor of God so that you can fight
against the devil's evil tricks.
Our fight is not against people on earth, but
against the rulers, authorities and powers of
this world's darkness, against the spiritual powers
of evil in this world.
Keep alert and pray; otherwise temptation will
overpower you.
For though the spirit is willing enough,
the body is weak.
Oh, what joy for those whose sin is put out of sight.
whose lives are lived in complete honesty.
When I refused to confess my sin, I was weak
and miserable, and I groaned all day long.
Day and night Your hand of discipline was heavy on me.
Finally I confessed all my sins to You and stopped
trying to hide them.
Therefore, let all the godly confess their sin while
there is still time, that they may not drown in
the flood waters of judgment."
I will guide you along the best pathway for your life;
I will advise you and watch over you."
Many sorrows come to the wicked but unfailing
love surrounds those who trust in the Lord.
So rejoice in the Lord and be glad, all you who
obey Him!And so my children, listen to Me, for happy
are all who follow My ways.

John 12:32

"And I, if I be lifted up from the earth, will draw all men unto Me."

KEEP FOCUSED

Be careful that you be determined to follow God.
I must be first and foremost on your mind, then others.
Be mindful of My presence and purpose.
In every day happenings look to me, trust Me.
I am doing a perfect work in and through you to fulfill
My plan for you.
You are My servant, a servant's job is not easy?
A servant is subject to his master, obeys his commands,
You will not understand My ways, especially in using you with
and for others.
You must trust Me with each relationship you are
involved in. These are divine appointments.
You will touch lives in My Name. You will cause others
to notice that I am working in their lives; and bring
their focus back to me and not all the stuff that is going on
around them.
For I am not where I should be in many of My people's
lives that you will encounter for Me. You will know what to say.
My Holy Spirit will prompt you.
Most importantly you must realize that it is your very
commitment and devotion to Me that will draw others to Me.
But some will turn away from you, because they want their own way.
My Holy Spirit in you turns the light on their wrong doing,
sometimes without you saying a word.
Walk away, let go and leave them for the Holy Spirit to
do His work in them.
You life radiates My presence when you spend much time
with Me in prayer and devotion to the work I have called you to do.
It is who you serve, you become master to.

Romans 12:12

"Rejoicing in hope; patient in tribulation,;
continuing instant in prayer…"

KEEP SILENT AND HOLD FAST

Listening is most important as you speak with others.
Remember they may be hurting at this time
And this tends to make them center on self.
That is the enemy's way of getting their focus off the God who created them.
The 'woe is me' syndrome happens often.
Do not think about how people treat you,
Keep in mind that they may be going through a difficult time.
Your mind needs to be on ME always and My purpose for all things happening around you.
Listen, I say, to what folk are saying, if there is something you can do or say to help, by all means try.
If not, keep silent and just "be there";
and give all to Me in prayer.
Keep focused on the things of God and hold fast to your faith.
Though the rode be rough, encourage others to cling to My Truth as it will set them free.
My way is not burdensome, for I am the burden bearer.
Trust Me in all circumstances. Trust Me with all the people I place in your life, for they are there for a reason.
To fulfill the great commission—go forth and win the lost at any cost.
Watch and pray. Keep your heart and mind from the world and all its passions; and desire the righteousness that only I can give you.

1 Timothy 5:25

"Likewise, also the good works of some are manifest beforehand; and they that are otherwise cannot be hid."

KEEP STRONG SPIRITUALLY

You have read in My Word about My people becoming
lukewarm to the things of God.
This ought not to be.
It is too easy to get caught up in the things of this world,
and not give Me the time to work in your life, feed you
through My Word and help you grow spiritually.
Be careful, for even folk very close to you are able
to draw you away and entice you to compromise.
Remember, it takes discipline to be a disciple.
Stand fast and know I have brought you this far,
yet I have much more in store for you.
You have come to far to turn back now.
Listen for Me always, and obey My voice.
This is not the time for compromise, but for
perseverance in what you know I expect from you.
Be an example to others, be faithful in all that
I call you to do.
Be careful, I say again, to follow after Me
and My ways, to be a light in this dark world.
Trust that I am leading and guiding your steps.
Walk where I take you and show forth My glory
and love.

Mark 5:36

"As soon as Jesus heard the word that was spoken,
He saith unto the ruler of the synagogue,
Be not afraid, only believe."

LEAN ON ME

Circumstances and situations in life will try to rob you of feeling My presence.
Stand on the Word of God,
I will never leave you nor forsake you
I want you to lean on Me much more
in this world of the unknown.
You are not of this world, you are mine.
You know I have a path for you; so
desire to follow My leading.
Trust Me to do what I tell you I will do.
There are some things you will see and
understand in the Spirit, that others are unable to comprehend.
You see in part and you will know only in part—
yet you will see My Will come to pass.
This is what proves a true child of God.
Others may argue, yet they will see
when they also seek Me with all their heart.
I AM in control as you allow Me to be.
Trust Me completely and you will see in this day
and age many great and mighty happenings.
Go in My Name and because you believe,
others will know and receive.

Proverbs 1:5

"A wise man will hear, and will increase learning; and a man of understanding shall attain unto wise counsels."

LEARN OF ME

Do not question the steps I will have you take.
As in the past I have guided you one step at a time,
and you have followed Me.
Life is a walk of faith, and few there are who choose
to walk in it.
Most want to know what is in the future for them.
Yet that is not for them to know.
Live each day as I give it to you,
and watch new things continually open up.
I have always had a plan and purpose,
no matter where I've led you.
I am inspiring you even now in a new way.
Drink My Word in and learn of Me.
Experience anew; how I walked among my people
in ages before you.
Have I changed?
I change not.
I still desire my people to worship Me in
Spirit and in truth;
calling them to touch the lives of others
with my love and wisdom.
Go now, in newness of life.
Receive all I have to give you
in this life
and in preparation for the life to come.

Proverbs 3:26

"For the Lord shall be thy confidence,
and shall keep thy foot from being taken."

LET YOUR CONFIDENCE BE IN ME

I am taking you in a new direction, if you care to go with me.
Bringing you to a higher plain.
This spiritual adventure will be different.
You will experience a renewal in your spirit,
a spirit of trust…not in man, but in Me.
In all situations and circumstances happening henceforth,
you will be handling things with much more confidence.
Mainly because you will no longer look to yourself as to
how to respond or decide what to do, you will trust all to Me.
Knowing that I do all things well.
I will finish what I began in you.
I need you to be My light in this dark world more than
ever before.
I can only use a vessel who is completely
surrendered to Me and My purpose;
for much is to is to come to pass.
You will have peace though things around you and
that you hear about, confront you.
Follow Me and, as always, I will bring you victory
over many stumbling blocks that seem to get in your way.
I will keep him in perfect peace, whose mind is
stayed on Me,
because you trust in Me.

1 Peter 2:21

"For even hereunto were ye called: because Christ also suffered for us, leaving us an example, that ye should follow his steps."

LETTING GO

There is a way that seems right to man, yet it leads to destruction.
Life in the flesh is always contrary to a life being led by the Spirit.
This is the reason you must continue to learn and change.
The flesh always wants to dominate. This ought not to be.
When you yield all to Me, your God, that is the
only way I can take prominence in your life.
Then you will call upon Me in prayer, I will listen to you
and answer to what you ask of Me.
I have shown you My way many times and you have
followed by faith.
Do it now, though you cannot see what lies ahead.
I know you are unsure of exactly what is
happening right now; but have
confidence that I am working in your life.
Lean on Me and you will have no reason to doubt that
I am taking care of you.
Letting go means just that—believing that
I, your God, am always working in your life.
I will not allow My people who are
obedient to Me to fall.
I desire to lift you to higher places in Jesus
your Savior.
Follow My leading, for I am directing your path,
not man.

Romans 8:21

"Because the creature itself also shall be delivered
from the bondage of corruption
into the glorious liberty of the children of God."

LIBERTY AND JUSTICE FOR ALL

You know how I welcome you to come before Me with
quietness and openness of heart.
You will enter my presence and hear my voice.
It is so necessary to focus on the things of God
in your every day tasks.
For in the busy times of your day you will find yourself
mindful of me no matter what transpires.
This is because you have chosen to put Me, your God,
in right perspective in your life.
Center all around Me, the Lord and Savior of your very life.
I created you, chose you and set you apart that others may know
that I am God. To truly know Me in the fulness of My Spirit
is to know freedom and liberty.
There are many in the world carrying heavy
chains and yolks of bondage, only because
they choose to stay there.
They except it all as the way of life destined for them.
The father of lies deceives them and they believe him,
instead of the One True God who desires
and is able to set them free.
Oh that my people would put their very lives in My care;
and trust their Creator to do what He purposed to do in
and through them.
You are My people and when you entrust all to Me,
I will make myself known to you as
you experience great and wonderful
things that you cannot imagine. Yet you will know
that it was I who brought you out of darkness into
His marvelous Light to learn and know My plan
and purpose for you.

Colossians 3:17

"And whatsoever ye do in word or deed,
do all in the name of the Lord Jesus,
giving thanks to God
and the Father by Him."

LIFE IS A SPIRITUAL JOURNEY

Receive My refreshing touch today. As your latest journey has
been a rugged one. A journey of mixed emotions. You
realize that wherever you go and whoever you are with,
My work goes on.
It continues wherever I send you. You are My disciple—
do you see the importance of a disciplined life?
People are always watching how a Christian lives.
How they conduct their daily affairs.
What takes predominance is what really matters.
The things of God must matter most.
Oh, how the things of this world try to take precedence
even in believer's lives. Why do you suppose that is?
They seem to cater so to the flesh, when it is their spirits
that are really hungry.
Nothing else really satisfies, but for a brief time.
What is done for Christ lasts through eternity.
Though you feel you don't say much, your unspoken words
do much.
A mission is accomplished, a good work is done.
There is a time that I send you, for My will and purpose to be
accomplished in and through you.
As a result you will see the fruit of you labor.

Psalm 25:9

"The meek will he guide in judgment:
and the meek will he teach his way."

LISTEN AND HEED

You can do all things as you fully trust in Me
with expectation in your heart.
Show forth your faith as you lean on Me in every
circumstance in life.
As I lead you in a new direction, new path that you have
never been on, you feel the challenge.
Yet you also feel the excitement that this spiritual journey
always gives you.
Always pray for direction and instruction.
Remember, prayer is a two way conversation.
Take time to hear from me.
If you ask me to guide you, then not listen,
you will end up going your own way.
Wondering why things don't work out.
I am not that far away that you can't see my hand in
everything you are doing.
Yes, I am that close for you to hear me say,
"This is the way, walk ye in it."
Be confident of this very thing, what I have
called you to do,
I will give you the time and ability to do it.
Because you trust fully in Me, I will show you
the way, and you will walk in it and cause my
will to be done on earth as it is in heaven.

Numbers 23:26

"But Balaam answered and said unto Balak, Told not I thee, saying, All that the Lord speaks, that I must do?"

LISTEN TO ME

There are so many voices.
The world is full of people's opinions and thoughts
on who I am.
Also the voices of darkness, with the negatives and deception
try to bring confusion to My very elect.
There is only one voice that My people must listen for.
Seek Me with all your heart and you will find Me.
I am never too afar off.
Whenever you ask, I will speak and direct your steps.
Each day when you come to Me, I am waiting to listen
to all you have to say.
When you take time with Me, will I not come to you and grant
your desires?
I long for an intimate relationship with you.
A closeness that no one can sever.
There is much I have for you to do, as you seek My will each day.
I will open doors of opportunity for you to reach out
and touch the lives of others for My glory.
There is a hungry harvest, lost and dying, without hope.
Think about those I have brought into your life directly.
Be mindful of the calling in Christ Jesus for you to
disciple my People.
Encourage them to learn of Me while there is still time.
The harvest is ripe, but the laborers are few.
Let nothing hinder you from what I call you to do.
There is nothing so rewarding as serving your Living God;
and bringing others to accept the One True God who
longs to be their Savior and Lord.
Tell them Who I AM.

John 8:12

"Then spoke Jesus again unto them, saying,
I am the light of the world; he that
follows Me shall not walk in darkness, but
shall have the light of life."

LISTEN, I WILL TELL YOU

It is difficult in this world today to take the time
to hear Me speak to you?
Be careful that every day things do not take
you away from the very thing I have called
you to do and be.
I have given you gifts to be used,
(you are using one now) and time to
use them for my glory.
Be faithful in the little things I tell you to do;
and I will show you great and mighty things you
will accomplish in My name.
Do not weary in well doing, for I promise
to be with you always.
Be not anxious about anything.
All is in My hands. I will answer you in time.
Faith is the answer to many questions in life.
Faith helps you endure trials.
Faith bring you through to victory.
I have never let you down, there is a time and a season
for everything.
Take hold of your faith in Me and I
will bring this also to pass.
Look unto Me, the author and finisher of your faith.
You will see how your life is purposed to
glorify Me in all that you do.
God in My name and do all things as
I lead you.
I am your God and I love you.

John 16:24

"Hitherto have ye asked nothing in my name:
ask, and ye shall receive, that your joy may be full."

LIVE AND BREATHE IN ME

You come to me in Prayer and I know all that
is on your heart.
Yet I teach you to come to me with your needs and
the needs of others.
This way you will see My hand in everything
you bring to Me each day.
Ask, in humble expectation; knowing I will answer you.
Have confidence that whatever you ask, according
to My will, you will receive.
There is nothing I withhold from you, yet I require
obedience and devotion to what I call you to do.
Be faithful in reaching out to those I entrust to your care.
They need to learn how to plug into their
Source of Salvation to receive all I have for them.
There is so much My people miss when they do not humble
themselves and come away from their busy lives to sit at My feet.
Tapping into the Source of their Salvation
who longs to show them abundant life.
Enjoy all I give you here on earth, but always remember,
without Me you would have or be nothing.

2 Corinthians 1:3

"Blessed be God, even the Father of our Lord Jesus Christ, the Father of mercies, and the God of all comfort."

LIVE FREE

Do not wonder or fret when folk do not
experience peace and joy in their lives.
This is their problem, not yours.
Tell them the way of the Cross brings peace and joy.
It comes from within where My Spirit dwells
the believer.
Having your mind set on things above and your
whole being saturated with the anointing of
the Holy Spirit, allows you to experience this.
This is not an easy walk, yet the
joy of the Lord is your strength.
Folk filled with SELF are very difficult to be
around—but they won't want to be
around you either.
There is a part of them that truly hungers
for the freedom only Jesus can give.
This freedom only comes from true surrender.
Surrendering all that is selfish and self-centered
to become Christ centered.
When you allow Me the throne of your life,
you will see My will and purpose fulfilled.
I desire to guide every move you make and
will be glorified in all that you do.
Many do not understand the walk in the Spirit,
for it is beyond understanding.
It is a faith walk, trusting Me completely.
I AM your God and I care for you.

John 12:26

"If any man serve me, let him follow me;
and where I am, there shall also my servant be.
If any man serve me, him will my Father honor."

LOOK UNTO ME

My WORD is a lamp unto your feet and a light
unto your path, therein you will find life.
Spiritual nourishment is within it's pages.
Feed on My Word and receive the guidance,
strength, ability and wisdom to carry out My plan.
For you know My reason for creating this world was to
glorify My Father in heaven, your creator. He who
sent you His son, your Redeemer.
Yet few look to Me for life's directions, life's plan
from creation.
This is why the world is in turmoil, running to and fro
aimlessly.
Spending little time with the One who created them,
nor even wanting to know why they are here.
There is a way that seems right unto man, yet it leads
to destruction.
I desire to guide you, but you must choose to follow me.
Each day I have a plan for you, will you choose to seek it?
Trust and obey, for there's no other way, to be happy
in Jesus than to trust and obey.
A wonderful song, speaking truth.
I speak to you in many ways, are you listening?
You can trust Me with everything, especially entrust
your loved ones to Me.
For in this way God desires to work in and through
His people to build His kingdom.
The church, God's people are the only
means by way others will know and learn of Me.
Go forth now, the harvest is ready, plant the seeds
and reap the fruit of your labor for My glory.

Philippians 4:13

"I can do all things through Christ which strengthens me."

MUCH IS REQUIRED

Nothing is too difficult for Me.
When I call My people to a task, I also equip
them to accomplish it.
Everything that you do, I have a purpose for.
Your doubts and fears can hold you back.
You must venture out in faith, knowing you will finish
what you have begun.
Do not let anything hinder the tasks set before you.
Do not be so busy that you cannot perfect that which
I have called you to do.
Much is required of My people.
It is expedient that you spend much quiet time
with Me to hear from Me.
Do not be concerned with being busy, just
"being" who I made you to be.
I have a plan and purpose for you as a child of God.
The desires of your heart I have put there;
and you will see them fulfilled.
Remember, those who humble themselves
before Me, I will exalt in due time.
My Word shall not return void.
Everything you do in My name is for My glory.
Go forth and see what I will do for and with you.
Trust Me and walk with Me, I, your God
have ordered your steps; and desire to bless you.

Romans 6:4

"Therefore we are buried with him by baptism into death:
that like as Christ was raised up from the dead
by the glory of the Father, even so
we also should walk in newness of life."

MY DIVINE WILL

You say to Me, "so many changes!"
Yes…I know what you need to do to prepare for
each step I would have you take.
You need confidence to walk the walk I have prepared for you.
You are surprised when things you have asked for come
to pass. That is because all is done in My time,
not yours.
Life is so full of uncertainty.
You make decisions that seem good and right,
but then, in reality you say, this can't be right!
Of course it is, for I have allowed it for your good.
You will learn from all situations in life.
The flesh does not know how to walk in the Spirit.
It wants to have and do much that is against
My Spirit that dwells in you.
Rest in Me, I say, and you will not fulfill the lusts
of the flesh.
You will walk in newness of ife, and feel the
freedom of being in My divine will.
Some of what comes to you in My permissive will,
I allow that you may learn I desire you to walk in My
divine will.

Hebrews 3:7+8; Matthew 11:15

So, as the Holy Spirit says:
"Today, if you hear My voice,
do not harden your hearts…
He who has ears to hear,
Let him hear."

MY PEOPLE HEAR MY VOICE

I am the Creator of all things
There is nothing I can't do. Nothing is too difficult for me.
As you look to Me for answers in the natural,
there may not be any. That is why I ask you to walk by faith.
You do not have to be concerned with the outcome
of situations...give them to Me to work out.
Wait and see what I will have you do, or how
I use others to fulfill your needs.
My ways are not like your ways,
they are far beyond your human reasoning.
Wherever I lead you, the strength of your
obedience to Me will carry you through.
Have confidence in knowing your sensitivity to My Spirit.
Very few of My people give Me their undivided attention;
nor wait earnestly for Me to speak with them.
You have learned, My child, to discipline yourself;
for you desire with all your being to have
the same intimate relationship with Me,
that I so desire to have with you.
This is the only way your life can truly be fulfilled
in and through Me.
My people hear My voice and follow Me.

Psalm 37:7

"Rest in the Lord, and wait patiently for Him;
trust also in Him; and He shall bring
it to pass."

MY PRESENCE IS REFRESHING

Fret not about what is going on around you,
know that your are about your Father's business.
There is nothing too difficult for Me.
I am working in and through My yielded vessels
to bring forth My purpose for your life as well as others.
Rest in Me, trust in Me, follow Me.
Do not look to the left or to the right as I say in My Word,
You must keep your heart and mind stayed on Me.
Draw close to those who are hungering and thirsting
for righteousness.
I have put them in your life that you may build one
another's faith, as I use you to build My Kingdom.
Seek Me with all your heart, soul and mind, and you
will find me.
Deep in the recesses of your being is where I dwell.
You need to come aside to the holy place to listen
and learn of the deep things of God.
My presence is refreshing as you meditate on all
that you can be in Me.
Meditate on the instrument of peace you can be
because of My Spirit flowing through you.
I am all that you are and all that you ever will be.
I must be allowed to flow through you.
So be ever mindful of My indwelling presence
which brings forth living water for all who are thirsty.
Do not dwell on the circumstances in your life,
look to what I, your God, am doing and will do
on your behalf.

Jeremiah 33:3

"Call unto Me, and I will answer you,
and show you great and mighty things,
which you know not."

MY SPIRIT GUIDES

Do not weary in well doing. For what I call you
to do and be is not burdensome.
I have already equipped you to do it.
You must sacrifice and be diligent in the things
set before you.
Desire My will and you will walk in it each day.
Do not question the things that confront you.
I desire to show you how to handle everything life
brings to you.
Again I say, there is no need to struggle,
but yield to My Spirit who dwells within you.
I desire to bring forth truth in your inward parts.
In the deep recesses of your soul, you cry out
for spiritual nourishment.
Feed on My Word and you shall have
strength to endure.
Many answers will come to you from within
yourself as you yield all to Me.
I will always make things clear to you.
Whenever you ask, believe, trust and expect Me to answer.
I will show you, teach you, instruct you, guide you and
protect you.
Call on Me and I will answer.
You will see and learn that I desire the best for you;
and want to be an intricate part of you daily tasks…
only if you allow Me to be.

Psalm 119:103

"How sweet are thy words unto my taste!
yea, sweeter than honey to my mouth!"

MY WORD GIVES NEW LIFE

Wherever you go, whatever you do, I go
before you and prepare the way.
When your life is hid in Me,
My Holy Spirit flows through you.
My Word is nourishment to your soul,
strength to your very being.
Meditate on My Word. Drink in My promises
When you surrender your life to the God
of your Salvation, you become a partaker of
My Divine Nature.
My Word is life to you. Do not neglect it.
For in being diligent in reading it you will
feed the temple of My Holy Spirit,
which is your body.
Turn to Me often in your day to praise Me;
for I welcome the praises of my people.
Remember always, My Spirit is with you,
I go before you, I walk beside you,
I am holding your hand; and whenever necessary,
I even carry you at times.

Isaiah 55:11

"So shall My Word be that goes forth out of My mouth.
It shall not return unto Me void, but it shall
accomplish that which I please, and it shall prosper
in the thing whereto I sent it."

MY WORD SPEAKS LIFE

Listen to the quiet, it brings peace.
Appreciate the solitude and warmth of My presence.
It is good and wise to take time out in the world's busy
schedules to seek out a quiet and relaxed environment.
Be still and know that I am God.
This way you can always refocus your outlook on all situations.
As you work out your own salvation, with fear and
trembling, you must rely on Me.
For without Me, your efforts are in vain,
This world, Satan and even self is wanting to dominate
your life; so continually submit all to Me.
There is no other way, but to forfeit all for what I would
have you to do and be.
You will want for nothing, because you trust in Me.
All is given to you that I may be glorified in and through you.
There is nothing you cannot accomplish in My Name.
Walk in that confidence.
Do not focus on circumstances around you, focus on Me.
I am doing a perfect work in and through you.
Read My Word prayerfully each day, as My Spirit
will teach you all things.
Scripture knowledge humbles, gives joy,
leads you nearer to God, and is not easily reasoned
away, since we obtain it straight from God.
For you shall go our with joy, and be led forth with
peace. learning My Truths and being set free.
When others lives are touched; I will be glorified.

2 Peter 3:9

"The Lord is not slack concerning His promise,
as some men count slackness; but is
long suffering to us-ward, not willing
that any should perish, but that
all should come to repentance."

MY WORD WILL SET YOU FREE

My Word is a lamp unto your feet and a light unto your path.
Therein you will find life. Spiritual nourishment is within its pages.
Feed on My Word and receive the guidance, strength and ability
to carry out My purpose for your life.
I created this world to glorify your Father in Heaven,
Your Creator, Your Redeemer.
So few look to Me for life's directions, life's plan from creation.
This is why the world is in turmoil, running to and fro.
Spending little time with the One who created them,
nor even seeking why they were created.
There is a way that seems right unto man,
yet it leads to destruction. I desire to guide you,
but you must choose to follow My way.
Each day I have a plan for you…trust and obey, for
there's no other way to be happy in Jesus than to
trust and obey.
A wonderful song, speaking truth.
You must trust me with everything and entrust your
loved ones to me.
My people are the only means by way others will know
and learn of Me, the God of their Salvation,
Who longs to set them free.
Go forth now, the harvest is ready, plant the seeds
and reap the fruit of your labor for My glory.
My Kingdom come, My will be done on earth
as it is in heaven…

1 Peter 1:3

"Blessed be the God and Father of our
Lord Jesus Christ, which according to His
abundant mercy hath begotten us again
a lively hope by the resurrection of
Jesus Christ from the dead."

MY WORD—YOUR LIGHT

Wherever you go, whatever you do, I go before you and
prepare the way.
When your life is hid in Me, My Holy Spirit
flows through you.
In this way I fulfill My purpose in all that I would
have you do.
My Word is nourishment to your soul,
strength to your very being.
Meditate on My Word. Drink in My promises.
When you surrender your life to Me, you become
a partaker of My divine nature.
Yes, the blood of My Son Jesus Christ cleanses
you from all sin.
He bore your sins in His body on the cross,
that you might die to sin and come alive unto righteousness.
for by His wounds, you are healed.
My Word is life to you, do not neglect it.
For to be diligent in reading My Word, you will feed the
temple of My Holy Spirit, which is your body.
It not only needs physical food, but spiritual
nourishment to survive.
This is a spiritual journey on this earth.
I am with you always, be ever mindful of My presence.
Turn to Me often in your day to praise Me.
For I welcome the praises of My people.
Remember, My Spirit is with you, I go before you,
I walk beside you, and I am holding your hand
when necessary…I even carry you at times.

GALATIANS 6:9+10

"And let us not be weary in well-doing: for
in due season we shall reap, if we faint not.
As we have therefore opportunity, let us
do good unto all men, especially unto them who
are of the household of faith."

NEW LIFE

Your faithfulness in wanting to obey Me
will always bring forth fruit.
My ways are beyond your understanding that is why
it takes faith and trust to accomplish those tasks
I put before you.
My Spirit dwells in you and will prompt you,
and always help you discern what is not pleasing to Me.
You feel what I feel when you experience the
enemy in control.
I grieve for My people, but I am also angry.
They allow much to come into their lives
and control them.
I desire to strip them of their old ways,
desires and habits.
I say to you, Put on the new man, yet they choose
to stay in bondage to the old.
Do you realize that what I have for you is so much
better than all you hold on to in this world.
The things of this world only hold you captive.
All that is not of Me and for My glory will
keep Me from intervening in your life.
I desire to set My people free; but you must
freely choose to surrender all to Me.
Things of this world will soon pass, only what's
done for Christ will last.
Allow your God to give you new life
forgive you and and allow Jesus Christ to
be Lord and Savior of your life.

Jeremiah 6:16

"Thus saith the Lord, Stand ye in the ways, and see,
and ask for the old paths, where is the good way,
and walk in them, and ye shall find rest for your souls..."

ONE RIGHT CHOICE

Faithfulness, faithfulness is what I long for.
Faithfulness is what I call you to.
When you are faithful to the things of God,
all circumstances will work out for good.
As you put your trust in Me, you cannot help but
see My hand in every facet of life.
You then see with My perspective, not your own.
In everything here on earth, I have a part.
All I have created, I can control.
There is a problem only when My people want their own way.
In everything, there is only one right way, one right choice.
All the answers are in My Word and come
through prayer.
Do I not say, "This is the way, walk ye in it?"
Yes, the answers to life are very simple when you trust Me.
Yet, human nature always wants to make it complicated.
If what you want to do does not line up with My Word,
and bring peace, it is not what I would have you do.
When I guide you, there will be no confusion.
The peace that passes all understanding will be your guide.
I do not cause division…what I have brought
together, let no man separate.
Watch and pray that you might know My will.
Wait on the Lord, for not every door that opens is My way.
Seek peace with everything you venture to do.
I AM the God of peace, seek Me with all your heart
and I will direct your path.
Wait, I say, on the Lord and you will always know
what to do, where to go and with who.

2 Thessalonians 2:2

"That ye be not soon shaken in mind or be troubled, neither by spirit, nor by word, nor by letter as from us, as that the day of Christ is at hand."

ONLY ONE VOICE

There are many voices in the spiritual realm, but
only one Who speaks absolute truth.
Coming before Me often will teach you how
to be sensitive to the voice of the Holy Spirit
from within you.
Your spirit will bear witness to the prompting of the
Holy Spirit, and you will follow My leading.
Just as you write with confidence, as you journal
your thoughts, you will also know what to
say to others.
Listen, as others speak, and I will give the when
and what to say, if anything.
Wait on Me, I say, in every situation.
Remember, you cannot draw others to Me, lest the
Holy Spirit from within is allowed to reach out to them.
Waiting is very difficult, but I must have time to prepare
their hearts to receive what My people have to say.
The flesh must die before the spirit can truly come alive
and be fruitful.
Whoever you are with, pray and seek to be
yielded, that I may flow through you for the work
being done in the lives around you
in My Name and for My glory.
Go forth in My Name and because of your faith,
others will learn and be saved.

Job 22:21+22

"Acquaint now thyself with Him, and be at peace:
thereby good shall come unto thee.
Receive, I pray thee, the law from His mouth,
and lay up His words in thine heart."

OUR FATHER'S BUSINESS

Sometimes you get so very busy.
Yet, always keep in mind to be busy about your
Heavenly Father's business. Being ready to tend to the
needs of others, those unable to do for themselves,
before your own,
Also learning, that you be more knowledgeable
about the things of God, and useful in witnessing to
those around you about Me, the God of their salvation.
Keep your mind stayed on Me, and My plans
for you each day.
It is good to be busy in what I have called you to do.
Each day is a challenge, at all times being prepared
for whatever I have in store for you.
It will always be easy to accept; and you will have peace
in the recess of your mind and heart that
you are to do or stop doing something, even when
your flesh doesn't want to.
Keep your eyes on the high calling in Christ Jesus,
and reach for the prize.
Your reward is great when you deny yourself for
the work of My Kingdom.
Yet you will also receive blessings as you go
forth in My Name.
Always mindful that whatever time you spend
in My service will be fruitful for the day.
I am with you always, when you speak with Me
during your busy day...I will hear you and
I will answer.
Go and evangelize the world with My love and truth.

John 1:1

"In the beginning was the Word, and the Word was with God, and the Word was God."

OUR GREAT COMMISSION

You have completed many things so far in your lifetime.
Each task finished brings a new beginning.
Yielding to Jesus is what you need to do continually.
It is My way that will produce fruit.
How do you know you are in My will and
doing things My way?
My peace goes with you, and you will not be moved.
As you walk in the Spirit you will reap a harvest for Me.
My people who are called by My name, humble themselves
and pray.
These are those who will have a following after them.
They will see results in all that they seek to
accomplish in My name.
Your life will go forth into this dark world
as a light for others to see and find their way to Me.
Your desire to teach and encourage others is strong.
Know that this is what I have called the older
women to do; the younger are to listen and learn.
Your very countenance shows forth My light.
It is I who people see in You.
They know when My servants have been in the
presence of their God.
Bask in My presence often, for there you will
receive rest and strength to carry the great commission
to those around you.
Tell them I love them, and I desire to draw them close to Me.
Encourage others to come and I will receive them
and give them new life in Me.

Isaiah 48:17

"Thus saith the Lord, thy Redeemer, the Holy One
of Israel; I AM the Lord thy God which
teaches thee to profit, which leads thee
by the way that thou should go."

PERFECT PEACE

My great desire is to answer prayer that I may be glorified.
I am your burden bearer.
Cast all your cares on Me, for I care for you.
If you ask for bread, will I give you a stone?
No, of course not.
Ask and you shall receive, seek and you shall find.
All your needs will be met,
and you will always find direction.
Yet you must seek My will.
Your requests, when in line with My will for you,
will always be fulfilled.
If you have to wonder if something is My will or not,
wait on Me.
Wait for that peace to come regarding your decisions.
My way always brings forth fruit and growth
within yourself and others.
I use everything you do and learn, for then
I will shine from you in all your accomplishments.
So whatever you put your mind and heart to do,
do it all for My glory.
Each day seek My will. My spirit will direct you.

Psalm 16: 8+9

"I have set the Lord always before me; because He is at my right hand, I shall not be moved. Therefore my heart is glad, and my glory rejoices; my flesh also shall rest in hope."

POWER OF THE HOLY SPIRIT

Have I not always guided you through difficult
decisions in your life?
Call on Me and I will answer.
Ask and you shall receive.
I teach you the way to seek My will,
yet so many times you struggle through without
coming to Me.
You worry and wonder about what to do.
This is your human nature.
I desire you to walk in the supernatural
power of the Holy Spirit.
Knowing and experiencing My constant strength
and guidance to walk the walk I have
purposed for you.
I will never leave you nor forsake you, for I
have promised you this.
You are mine because you gave yourself to Me.
You struggle and have confusion only
because you want and think you have to be in
control of your own life.
If it is not your own to control, so let
your God do what He wants and needs to do
to fulfill your destiny and glorify the
Father who is in Heaven.
Go forth now and do what I have called you
to do and be.
Drawing all men unto Me,
as you go where I lead you and love
My people back to Me.

Luke 1:79

"To give light to them that sit in darkness, and in the shadow of death, to guide our feet into the way of peace."

PRAY WITH EXPECTATION

As you walk the pilgrim path, your faith is
renewed daily.
This is why you must turn to Me in every situation.
There is much you cannot handle yourself
in the human realm.
It takes the Holy Spirit working in and through
you to solve the problems of life.
Leave it with the Lord, you say…take it to the Lord
in prayer.
But, do you leave it there and wait in
expectation for Me to intercede and answer?
Yes, at times you do and you are blessed.
Yet, be careful that you do not take it back,
and begin to fret, worry, doubt or even
manipulate an answer for yourself.
When you come to Me in prayer…leave it there.
It is all in My hands now to do something about it.
Will I not do what you ask?
I desire nothing but the best for you.
I will shield you as you put your trust in Me.
If you worry, you are not trusting, but
when you are trusting, you have nothing
to worry about.
Walk in confidence, knowing you have put your God
in control of the situation.
I want nothing more than to lead and guide you in
all that you do each day.

Philippians 4:19

"But my God shall supply all your need according to His riches in glory by Christ Jesus."

PRAYER IS POWERFUL

You plant seeds, another waters, and I, through the
Holy Spirit, brings the increase.
Whenever you speak of Me or bring attention to Me
to others, you glorify your Father in heaven.
Lift Me up, I say, and I will draw all men unto Me.
There is a work to be done.
My Word must be brought forth with power from on high.
My anointing is upon My people to speak the Word
and tell My Truths at every opportunity.
Remember, whatever I call you to do, I have already
equipped you to do it.
There is a time and season for everything.
You will know what I will have you do,
as you allow Me to direct your steps each day.
Be My willing and available vessel, ready to be
poured out to others.
The world is full of needy people, meet them at their
need and show them how I long to fulfill their lives.
Their greatest need is to learn of Me and My ways
through reading and applying the Word of God.
Read how My presence moved mighty men of God
throughout the Bible stories.
As I was with them, I am with you through
the presence of the Holy Spirit in you.
That same power will move you as you
trust I will use you. Go forth into all the world
and teach what you have learned of Me; and you will bear
much fruit for My Kingdom.

1 John 5:14

"This is the confidence we have in approaching God:
that, if we ask anything according to His will,
He hears us."

PUT ALL YOUR TRUST IN ME

There is no better time than the present to bring
your deepest needs to Me.
At times you are not even sure nor how
some of your personal needs will ever be met.
Know that I am always near you.
All you ever need is to draw near to Me.
I know exactly what you are going through.
Trust in Me as I guide your steps
one day at a time.
You will know what to do in every situation
that confronts you.
Remember where I have brought you from
and what I have already done in your life.
Your faith in Me has made you strong.
Depend on your spiritual strength to bring you
through to victory again.
My will shall be done for that which you desire.

1 John 4:13

"Hereby know we that we dwell in Him,
and He in us because He hath given us
of His Spirit."

REACH THE LOST

It is only by faith that you experience the supernatural
life of Christ that is to be shared with others.
I will always give you the words to speak, so do not hesitate
to tell everyone in your path the good news of salvation.
Freely given to set man free from the condemnation that
is in this world.
My power is within you, you speak the oracles of
Almighty God because My anointing is upon you.
"Greater is He who is in you, than he who is in the world.
My Word will go out with power if My people will speak
out with boldness the words I give them to speak.
This is an individual, personal spiritual journey.
Each person is approached in a unique way.
I will show you the way to reach the lost; for I long
for them to come to Me.
Be a willing, obedient, open vessel so I may flow
through you.
Let your heart be open to the needs of others,
and tell them I am here to meet them.
My arms are outstretched to receive them into my fold.
I am the Great Shepherd and they will be My sheep.
I will lead and guide them into all truth
for I love them and care for them.

Romans 10:9

"That if thou shalt confess with thy mouth the Lord Jesus, and shalt believe in thine heart that God has raised Him from the dead, thou shalt be saved."

REAL EXPECTATIONS

It is so good that you come to Me to not only pray,
but to also expect to hear from Me.
I love to speak to My people; I need to speak to you.
Yet, so few take time to be quiet enough to hear.
You are seeing how I long to bless those who are
truly surrendered to Me.
You know that whatever happens to you that My
hand is in it.
Many are watching you and your total reliance on
your Heavenly Father.
The big difference that you have found, and many
have not, is that when you pray...you also expect.
You have a strong expectation that I will answer.
Well, why wouldn't I?
I want the best for My People, and I know what is best.
When you seek God's best, you will
receive it.
I have put you in this world to shine forth
My light into the darkness.
I have equipped you with My Spirit's power.
You will go forth in My Name and raise
up more disciples as I build
My kingdom through My faithful
servants.
Because you believe, others will know and be saved.

Hebrews 12:10

"For they verily for a few days chastened us
after their own pleasure; but He for
our profit, that we might
be partakers of His holiness."

Receive My Blessing

Building My kingdom. Think about it.
What builds My kingdom? My people do.
Is there any better way to go than My way?
Is there any better path to choose, than the path
I have already purposed for you?
Then why do you not follow Me?
Because you do not fully know and believe who I am!
You must fully know and believe in your heart all
I am capable of doing through and for you.
When you do, you will experience the window of
Heaven open unto you.
It is the obedient who receive My blessings;
for to be obedient is being in my divine will.
To see My hand in everything around you.
Holiness is what you long for, and is what others
see radiate from your very being.
This is why I have made you sensitive to the
response of others.
If they reject you, they reject Me, for you are My
representative in this world.
You are light, and darkness no longer remains in My light.
Those who choose to stay in darkness refuse to come
into My light for it shows forth their weaknesses.
Yes, I desire to be their strength in all matters of life.
I have come that they might have life.
Believe in Me, trust in Me, for I am the God of
the possible…I do all things well and for the good
of my people.
"Believe, obey and expect to see all I can do in and
through those who put their faith and trust in Me,
the God of all creation."

John 8:31+32

"Then said Jesus to those Jews which believed on Him.
If ye continue in My Word, then are
ye My disciples indeed;
And ye shall know the truth, and the truth shall
make you free."

REDEEM YOUR TIME

Do you notice that everything has a time?
Yet there is also an end to time—time on this earth.
It is so necessary to redeem the time.
Redeem the time you spend with your Lord and Savior.
Doing things as I lead you to do them.
My work must take priority for that is what truly matters.
Building yourselves up in the faith to equip you for
all that lies ahead for you to accomplish for Me.
As you are observing, there is much SELF inflicted problems
in the world and also in the churches today.
My church (My people) need to be Christ Centered.
The world, self and the devil need not rob My people, lest
they allow them to take rule in their lives.
I cannot set My people free, if they do not allow Me to.
They choose to allow other things or people to control and
influence them. My grace is sufficient.
Surrender all to Me.
I desire to direct your lives and meet your needs.
I am a blessing God.
I promise an abundant life, but few will find it.
Reach out with expectation to receive.
You rob yourselves of My fullness, but yes,
to receive this will take your time,
Come to Me often, allow me to refresh you in My Word.
Then you will be able to receive the promises of God,
which I long to bestow upon My people.

Romans 15:4

"For whatsoever things were written aforetime were written for our learning, that we through patience and comfort of the Scriptures might have hope."

RENEW YOUR FAITH

You have come so far, My child, in expectation of My will
being done when you ask. This is faith.
You also acknowledge that My ways are not your ways.
Notice how I bring things to pass, as this life is filled with
times of waiting, your faith is renewed and strengthened.
What you cannot do, you must leave with Me.
Yes, I am able to fulfill all that you ask and desire for
others; but you must remember I am working with
people in ways you do not know.
People of strong wills and hard hearts.
I will not break their wills. They must desire
to surrender all to Me.
I do not break hearts, their own rebellious nature causes this.
Even then, many do not turn to Me that I may put
the pieces back together.
Instead they become more calloused, where My love is
unable to penetrate and soften their hearts.
This ought not to be. These are the reason many are
troubled and sick.
They do not know to ask Me or expect
Me to help set them free,
so they ask amiss, with a doubting heart.
Your hearts and minds need reminding to focus on
their all mighty, all powerful God who is able
to do ALL things.
All I need is willing, surrendered vessels
to spread the Word,
that I am God and am calling them to come to Me.
Just as they are, I will receive them and
give them new life in My Son Jesus.

Psalm 51:10+11

"Create in me a clean heart, O God; and
renew a right spirit within me.
Cast me not away from Thy presence; and
take not Thy Holy Spirit from me."

RESTORE THE JOY

So many of My people are doing their own thing.
They are not seeking My will each day.
They do not truly believe that only My way works.
Things do not have to be the way they are…
turmoil, confusion and indecision.
This is why I have called on those who are
spiritually mature to teach and restore the younger.
They must teach all they have learned from
their experiences in this life.
Many are caught up in their difficulties and problems.
This ought not to be. Their focus must be on Me.
The world and its demands are robbing them
from My peace and My power.
There is power in prayer; for when you pray,
you are communicating with your Heavenly Father.
I AM your all knowing, all powerful God.
I know what is best, but you must seek Me with all your heart.
Then you will know how to live.
Why do you neglect so great a salvation?
I have set you free, so flee from the bondage
of this world and Satan.
Do not let anything rob you from your
time with God, this is essential.
As you devote your time, you learn of Me
and My ways come clearer.
You need to experience the power of My resurrection.
To do this you need to seek Me first, early in your day.
I must be first and foremost on your mind,
then I can restore the Joy of your Salvation.

Matthew 6:33

"But seek ye first the Kingdom of God and
His righteousness; and all these things
shall be added unto you."

SEEK LIFE

Be gentle with yourself. Am I, your God, gentle with you?
I am taking care of you. I desire to meet your every need and
the desires of your heart;
planning a support system all around you.
People who know and understand.
I am showing you my world. People can destroy people,
but only if you allow them to.
Allow is the important word; for what and how you allow
life and people effect you, it will be effected.
Leave behind those things that lead to destruction, and
follow after life.
The life I have purposed for you.
I am the way, the truth and the life.
You have come to the truth, now walk in the way
I shall lead you each day.
As you turn every thing over to Me, you will see
My hand and feel my presence working on your
behalf.
Trust in Me only and fully, and those you know I have
brought into your life to encourage
your spiritual journey.
I desire for you to fulfill your destiny in this life.
Let nothing or no one discourage your hope in Me.
I am the author and finisher of your faith.
Trust Me and see what will come out of your
obedience to me.

Psalm 27:13+14

"I had fainted, unless I had believed to see
the goodness of the Lord in the land
of the living.
Wait on the Lord; be of good courage, and
He shall strengthen thine heart:
wait, I say, on the Lord."

SEEK ME DAILY

You have many people on your heart today.
Bring them to me in prayer.
So many concerns in this fast moving world.
It seems that many do not want to slow down enough
to find Me in the midst of all their turmoil.
Oh, they think they have it all under control, yet
lest they allow Me to be in control of their lives—
all is hit or miss.
I purposed for all to need Me to be Lord of their lives.
This life here on earth cannot be lived
fully without their seeking My divine purpose.
It is so important the My people who are
called by My name humble themselves and pray.
Seek Me daily so I may guide and use you.
There is death all around you, spiritual death.
True life is only found in Jesus Christ.
I am the way, the truth and the life.
Come unto Me all ye who are heavy laden and
I will give you rest.
Rest from the burdens of this life, and yet
also a strong desire to reach the lost at any cost.
Go into all the world and speak the good news
to those who will hear.
Be willing and I will use you and give you
the words of Truth to tell them.

Luke 11:13

"If you then, being evil, know how to give good gifts unto your children: how much more shall your Heavenly Father give the Holy Spirit to them that ask Him?"

SEEK ME DILIGENTLY

Do you not desire all that your Heavenly Father
wants to give you?
You wonder what life in the Spirit is all about;
yet why do you not seek Me with your whole
heart, mind and soul?
I not only spoke through the prophets of old,
but through all who will yield themselves to Me.
I desire to work through you in accomplishing
My work on earth, when you allow Me to do so.
The promise of the Holy Spirit in Acts 2:39 is
given to all who accept God's call to
repentance and salvation through
Jesus Christ, our Savior.
How can you understand the things of God
lest the Spirit of God dwells in you.
As you accept Me as Lord of your life;
I am calling you out of this world of darkness
into My glorious light.
I will use you in ways you have ever imagined possible.
New life in Christ awaits you.
Come unto Me, trust Me to
instruct you in all My ways.

John 4:23

"But the hour cometh, and now is,
when the true worshipers shall worship the Father
in spirit and in truth:
for the Father seeks such to worship Him."

SEEK ME EARLY

You look at the trees around you, they all seem to be
reaching out and up, and continuing to grow.
I desire My people to desire to do the same.
Reach out and up to Me, the Savior of their lives.
I AM your strength.
Where are you looking to seek that joy and
peace only I can give you?
I am ministering to My people more in this present time
than ever before.
I want to be your fortress and keep you
protected from the attacks of the enemy of your soul.
Draw near to Me and the Body of Christ;
that you may stand accountable and stay in the truth.
I AM the way, the Truth and the Life.
No one comes to the Father than through Me.
This world is too busy to take time with Me.
I am a personal God and I care for you.
I bring My people into your life to help you grow.
Realizing the day is here when even My people
will fall by the wayside.
Desire to know My will and plan for you and to use you.
This takes total commitment with sacrifice.
Sacrificing your will for Mine.
I know what is best for you and want the best for you.
Seek Me early while I may be found,
and you will find the way to
pure joy and contentment in the Holy Spirit,
as I AM in the Father and the Father is in Me,
so I AM in you.

2 Corinthians 5:10

"For we must all appear before the judgment
seat of Christ; that every one may receive the things done
in his body, according to that he hath done, whether
it be good or bad."

SEEK MY DIRECTION DAILY

There is much in this world to be concerned about.
There are problems all around.
Most is caused by selfish ambitions.
There is cause to worry when folk are not seeking
My will for their lives.
They run to and fro, here and there, not having a clue
as to what I would have them do or not do.
My people know My voice and heed My call.
they long to learn My way and seek My direction.
I have a plan for the life I have given you.
I have given everyone free wills, they
must choose to follow Me.
Many are called, but few are chosen.
Yet because they want their own way or they
allow Satan to rob, steal and try to kill them.
There is a way that seems right unto man, yet
it leads to destruction.
Be careful to speak truth, be not concerned
about the responses of man.
Only the truth will set them free from the
bondage of sin and shame.
If there is anything I am not in control of and that
man has not been able to put under subjection,
then it is sin.
Be not enslaved to the yolk of bondage.
I have come that they may be set free.
Tell them to forsake all that binds them to this world,
and receive the freedom of My Spirit through
Christ their Lord.

Proverbs 4:20+22

"…attend to my words; incline thine ear
unto my sayings. Let them not depart from
thine eyes; keep them in the midst of thine heart.
For they are life unto those that find them,
and health to all their flesh."

SEEK MY INDWELLING PRESENCE

Fret not about what is going on around you.
Know that you are about your Father's business.
Rest in Me, trust in Me, follow Me.
Do not look to the left or to the right.
You must keep your heart and mind stayed on Me.
Deep in the recesses of your
being is where I dwell.
My presence is refreshing as you meditate on
all that you are, all that you can be and
the instrument of peace
I want you to be for others.
I must be allowed to flow through you.
Be mindful of my indwelling presence
which brings forth
Living Water to all who are thirsty.

2 Thessalonians 1:12

"That the name of our Lord Jesus Christ may be glorified in you, and ye in Him, according to the grace of our God and the Lord Jesus Christ."

SEEK TO BE YIELDED

There are many voices in the spiritual realm, but
only one Who speaks absolute truth.
Coming before Me often will teach you how
to be sensitive to the voice of the Holy Spirit
from within you.
Your spirit will bear witness to the prompting of the
Holy Spirit, and you will follow My leading.
Just as you write with confidence, as you journal
your thoughts, you will also know what to
say to others.
Listen, as others speak, and I will give the when
and what to say, if anything.
Wait on Me, I say, in every situation.
Remember, you cannot draw others to Me, lest the
Holy Spirit from within is allowed to reach out to them.
Waiting is very difficult, but I must have time to prepare
their hearts to receive what My people have to say.
The flesh must die before the spirit can truly come alive
and be fruitful.
Whoever you are with, pray and seek to be
yielded, that I may flow through you for the work
being done in the lives around you
in My Name and for My glory.
Go forth in My Name and because of your faith,
others will learn and be saved.

1 Corinthians 2:13

"Which things also we speak, not in the words which man's wisdom teaches, but which the Holy Ghost teaches: comparing spiritual things with spiritual."

SELF-CONTROL

Your life can be full when you desire
your spiritual life to have
dominion over life in the flesh.
The abundant life is not how much you gain in
worldly status or material possessions.
It is the rich abundance of the Spirit taking
residence in you; that lets you experience the
fullness of life only I, your heavenly Father,
can give you.
In all circumstances know that I have a
purpose to be fulfilled.
Look for My hand in every situation,
and ask Me to intervene before
you speak or do anything.
Take your time, listening as others talk with you.
Yield to Me, Then you will be able to
respond in the right spirit.
Listen, and if what they are saying
does not need an answer,
Do not be quick to give one.
Self-control is an important fruit to bear,
but you must apply it in all that you do.

Proverbs 3: 6+7

"In all thy ways acknowledge Him and
He shall direct thy paths.
Be not wise in thine own eyes;
fear the Lord, and depart from evil."

SHOW OTHERS THE WAY

Our God says, "Talk with Me today, for I love it when you do.
Then I know what is on your heart that you want Me to be a part of.
I love being included in your every day activities.
You are realizing now the importance of coming before me each day.
Humbly intercede in prayer for others like never before.
This world is evil and My people must humble themselves
and pray, that they may be ready at all times to give an
account of the faith that is within them through the Holy Spirit.
It is that power that will bring them through adversities.
Show others that I love them, care and desire to
help them also.
There is no other way to live this life in victory an peace
than through Christ your Savior.
Do I not care about you?
Did I not give My life for you to be set free?
Free for what?
To live this life in a way that glorifies Me.
In all your ways acknowledge Me
and I will show you the way.
I need My people to tell others the way;
for many are lost.
Any other ways are paths to destruction.
Choose you this day whom you will serve,
Christ or other idols?
Trust your life to Me, I long to forgive you and
set you free.
I will never leave you nor forsake you.
I love you with an everlasting love.

2 Thessalonians 2:13

"But we are bound to give thanks always to God for you, brethren beloved of the Lord, because God hath from the beginning chosen you to salvation through sanctification of the Spirit and belief of the truth."

STAND FIRM

I have led you to worship Me many different ways.
Think about your life thus far...What
was it that reached out to those around
you the most?
Your love for Me and your love for others.
It was always My hands extended through you
that drew others closer to Me.
Nothing has changed.
You are now choosing to worship Me in
Spirit and in Truth.
For you need only to be mindful of
My presence while worshiping Me.
Your thoughts are towards Me throughout your day.
Spiritual maturity is a deeper dependence on Me.
Your days are full because you allow Me
to fill them.
I have called you to a unique walk,
guided by the Holy Spirit.
By faith you will continue on the path
I have purposed for you.
You will see many doors of opportunity
open unto you.
Blessings upon blessings so that you may
in turn bless and reach out to others
in My name; and they may be
saved through the work of the
Holy Spirit to sanctify them, and
through belief in the truth.

Acts 19:20

"So mightily grew the Word of God and prevailed."

SPEAK MY WORD

There is so much going on around you, and so much to be done.
Yet you must look to Me at all times.
With great expectation you need to watch and wait.
Then and only then will you see that I am the
all mighty God of the universe.
Yes, my wrath is upon America. Many have forsaken Me.
This must not be—for I am their Creator.
How can anyone do anything proper without My intervention
in their lives.
My people have forgotten that I am the God of ALL creation.
They have tasted the disasters that are caused by those who
hate Me. Those who hate Me will hate you also.
They seek to harm those who desire peace. "My people who
are called by My Name must humble themselves and pray,
and seek My face more diligently than ever."
I will open more and more opportunities for those who will
speak My Word.
Go forth and make disciples. I need willing vessels
to go out and win the lost at any cost.
I will set the path and make the way if you will go
and do what I have called you to do.
Touch hearts I prepare for you and tell them
I love them.

2 Corinthians 5:15

"And that He died for all, that they which live should not henceforth live unto themselves, but unto Him which died for them, and rose again."

STRENGTH WITHIN

Resurrection…Just what does that mean to you?
The mysterious resurrection of Christ from the dead,
as well as the resurrected life His death gave us.
Yes, it is truly a mystery to all of us, but
by faith we can and will experience a
resurrected life; and walk in newness of life.
Accept and expect the transforming power of
the Holy Spirit to work in you.
Especially concerning your own behaviors
and habits with which you are displeased and know
do not please me.
Remember, I use everything for My glory.
As you continue to submit your own weaknesses to Me,
others see the continual changes manifested in your life;
as you allow Me to work in and through you.
Realize your human frailties, admit them, but do not
allow them to weigh you down.
Know that My yoke is easy and My burden is light.
Trust that I am working in you.
Remember that recognizing your weaknesses is the
first step to recovery.
Surrendering them, asking and expecting My strength to
help you overcome.
Wanting and excepting what I want for you, and recognizing
what others need is the walk of obedience.
J O Y=Jesus-Others-You
Walk in newness of life as you continually die to selfish
motivations and are risen in Christ Jesus who desires to
be Lord of your life, as long as you allow Him to be.

1 Peter 3:4

"But let it be the hidden man of the heart, in that which is not corruptible, even the ornament of a meek and quiet spirit, which is in the sight of God of great price."

SUBMIT ALL

There is nothing too difficult for God.
Look around you; there is sadness, sickness, oppression, depression and so much more keeping My people from the true expression of My Spirit within them.
Life is tough; that is why I gave My Son as the ultimate sacrifice for you.
Will you not do the same for me?
Life can be difficult, and at times it is you who make it so.
Doing things I have not meant for you to do.
Some people and situations you must entrust to Me totally; for there are times when you can interfere with my purpose for both you and them.
There are times when a situation occurs that I want you to submit to Me quietly and quickly; to allow Me to deal with it.
Especially in those circumstances when you feel your flesh rise and a wrong attitude begins to take over.
Then it is very necessary to pray and suppress the flesh.
This gives Me time to intervene, and My will to be done.
As I said, I desire to work out all things, when you are My willing vessel, yielded unto Me.
Your way does not work and never will.
Seek Me always and you will experience the peace that passes all understanding.

Romans 8:27

"And He that searches the hearts knoweth what is the mind of the Spirit, because He makes intercession for the saints according to the will of God."

TAKE MY HAND

Do you not see My hand in your life?
I know you very well, better than you know yourself.
When you have given your all to Me, will I
not take care of you?
I, alone, know what is best for you spiritually,
mentally, physically and emotionally.
I desire and will keep you on the path I purpose
for you; when you desire to walk with Me.
I have ordered the steps you are to take.
I know your every need, and I will meet it.
There are so many areas of life that demand
obedience.
I will always show you what you need to do.
You only need to choose to listen and obey.
You will reap the benefits from an obedient heart.
Your spirit will soar, your body will heal, your
emotions stable, our mind strong as it focuses
on God.
You see, I am with you always, my timing is
perfect in guiding you where you need to
be, to do what I need you to do, and to be
with who you need to be with.
All to accomplish My purpose on earth;
not only in your own life, but in the lives around you.
Your trust in Me will bring forth much fruit, as
you go forth in My Name and for My glory…
Remember, I go before you, so you must follow.

Romans 8:37

"...in all these things we are more than conquerors through Him that loves us."

TAKE STEPS OF FAITH

Change…So many do not like change in their lives.
Yet without change you will not move forward and
grow spiritually.
You must go where I lead and do as I instruct you to do;
for all things lead to life.
The life I have purposed for you.
I am directing your path because you have asked Me to.
Do not doubt the steps you are taking.
Though difficult at times and faith stretching, you know
I am with you always.
I will bring you through and you will experience
victory after victory.
Do not weary in well doing, for your faith will be stronger still,
because you fully trust in Me
for what seems impossible.
You will see how I continue to work all things together
for good for those who love Me and are called
according to My purpose.
Let your heart be light, as you continue
to trust Me to do what you desire.
For it is in your best interest that I have directed you this way.
As things come to pass, you will have seen My hand and
constant intervention in your life's journey.
Accept and enter into the abundant life.
For I am your God and I have promised this for you.
Be blessed and go forth in My name and bless others.

Proverbs 16:3

"Commit thy works unto the Lord, and thy thoughts shall be established."

TELL THEM WHO I AM

Do not question why others have needs and you have plenty.
You will have peace whenever I put it on your heart to give.
There will be no questions as to what you need to do
for them.
Many find themselves in difficult circumstances because
they have put themselves there.
Running to and fro with no real direction with the
enemy of their souls on their tail to lead them
down the path of destruction.
How can you help them, if I can't.
They do not seek Me or My help.
You are only expected to turn their focus to Me
For without Me they can do nothing.
When self in on the throne of their lives, then
I cannot be. I desire to direct their steps, yet
they choose to walk alone. Then they wonder why
nothing works out for them.
I am the God who created you, I know you better
than you know yourself. I know what is best for you.
Stand back and wait on Me when you have delivered
the Truth of My Word to others.
Trust in Me for I have told you of the ways I will
use you. You may not understand or see the
fruit of your labor for a time.
Yet, My Word never returns void. A seed planted will
always bring forth fruit in time; depending on the
soul in which it was planted receives it.
Your only concern and responsibility is to be
obedient in speaking forth My Word, not
how or if it is received.
You are my vessel, I know how I want to use you.

Romans 6:23

"For the wages of sin is death; but
the gift of God is eternal life
through Jesus Christ our Lord."

THE GREATEST GIFT

I, your God, gave My all; My only Son, Jesus Christ.
The gift of salvation that you might have eternal life.
Do not look to the world for the abundant life, for it
is in and through Me that you will find it.
This is the reason I call you out to be separate
from those choosing the "world's" way of life.
Come out from among them, I say, and be ye separate.
Be different, you ask? Yes, My ways are not of this world.
Your interests will no longer be earthbound, but heavenward.
I must become your reason for living.
My purpose for your life must take priority.
Learn of me and know My ways, ye who desire
my great Salvation and all that comes with it.
For My sheep hear My voice and follow Me.
The power of My Holy Spirit will control
your members as you yield yourself completely to Me.
Surrender means your all is given freely,
desiring only My will.
Nothing else matters, but to be in My divine plan for you.
You will see My hand in every situation,
because you are looking for Me.
Expect Me to show you the way.
Expect to receive the answers to every need,
solution to every problem;
and choose the path I have chosen to lead you through
to a victorious life.
Put all your trust in your Lord and Savior,
Author and Finisher of your faith.
My gift to you is everlasting life to all who believe.

Proverb 8:32

"Now therefore hearken unto me, O ye children:
For blessed are they that keep my ways."

THE KINGDOM OF GOD IS WITHIN YOU

Put on the full armor of God
so that you can fight against the devil's evil tricks.
Our fight is not against people on earth,
but against the rulers and
authorities and powers of this world's darkness,
against the spiritual power of evil in the heavenly world.
Keep alert and pray.
Let all the godly confess their rebellion to the Lord
while there is time, that they may not drown in
the flood waters of judgment.
Your Lord says, "I will guide you along the best
pathway for your life. I will advise you
and watch over you.
May sorrows come to the wicked,
but unfailing love surround those
who trust the Lord."
Rejoice in the Lord and be glad,
all you who obey Him!
NO HILL IS TOO HIGH,
NO MOUNTAIN TOO TALL,
FOR WITH FAITH IN THE LORD
YOU CAN CONQUER THEM ALL.

Acts 2:42

"And they continued stedfast in the apostles' doctrine
and fellowship, and in breaking of bread,
and in prayer."

THIS IS PRAYER

Prayer-Praying-Communicating with your God.
Just what do you think when you hear those words?
Every day is different and busy.
You are home—the phone rings—you're connected
and I am in your midst as always.
Was the call purposed to meet a need you have
or the one I connected you with,
or maybe both of you?
Sometimes you'll know, at times you won't.
Think about this…I always bring people together
to meet their innermost needs.
In such a time as this, listen to your heart, speak to me often
anytime, all the time throughout your day.
I am always with you to listen to you and hear your words.
THIS IS PRAYER.
I love the times you get away alone and commune with Me.
This is when I have your undivided attention.
Remember, you ALWAYS have Mine.
You may think you have nothing to give others, or not
receiving anything from others I put in your path.
My Spirit is flowing through you.
I have gifted you with much to share with one another.

Matthew 6:10

"Thy kingdom come. Thy will be done in earth,
as it is in Heaven."

THY KINGDOM COME

I know your innermost thoughts, the very
intent of your heart.
That is where lies the true desire to serve Me;
to become what I purposed you to be and do
from the beginning.
The life which I have given you is a life dedicated to Me.
As long as you choose My will, you will have
confidence in all that you do and say.
For I have made you a vessel of honor for Myself.
It is My work in and through you which makes
you fit for the Master's use.
Boldly write with confidence as it is I who speaks
the oracles of God to you.
I need your spirit to be an open source
by which I may flow.
All that you do will receive my anointing.
It is My Holy Spirit who flows through you
to work my perfect work in
an imperfect world.
I desire to use you to build the Kingdom of God on earth.
Do the things I set before you with great fervor,
to glorify Me.
Go in My Name ad because you believe,
others will know and be blessed.

1 Thessalonians 5:21-23

"Prove all things; hold fast that which is good.
Abstain from all appearance of evil.
And the very God of peace sanctify you wholly;
and I pray God your whole spirit
and soul and body be preserved
blameless unto the coming of our
Lord Jesus Christ."

THY WILL BE DONE

My child, I know exactly what you are going through.
It is difficult when dealing with the intimate
details of a relationship.
You can believe that I am in the midst of this,
because you have asked Me to be.
Do I not promise to lead you?
Do you believe that I am guiding you, even through this?
I allow everything in your life to perfect you for
what I have called you to do and be.
You are ever learning and coming to the
knowledge of your Lord and Savior.
I am always with you.
Though you fall you will not be cast down; I will lift you up
and bring you through.
Trust in Me as I guide you, one step at a time.
You will know what to do in every situation
Remember where I have brought you from.
Your faith in Me has made you strong.
Depend on your spiritual strength to bring you through
victoriously.
My will shall be done when it is your desire to follow Me.

Deuteronomy 8:3

"...That he might make thee know that man doth not
live by bread only but by every word that
proceeds out of the mouth of the Lord
doth man live."

THY WORD

My people are hungry for truth. My Word is truth.
In everything, seek My Word.
It is the road map to life.
Without it you will fail.
It is not just a ritual to open and read the Bible
and some magic will jump out to you.
You must study to show yourself approved unto Me, a workman
able to divide the Word of God.
Meditate on it day and night, that you may apply
it to your daily living.
When circumstances arise and decisions
are to be made, the Word of God is where to turn
for answers and direction.
Be diligent and faithful.
When you rely on Me, you are able to do all things.
Go forth in My Name, and the strength, wisdom and
ability will be there for you.
You confidence is in Me, for of yourself you can do nothing.
Trust and expect that whatever you ask of Me,
according to My will, you will receive.
For out of My abundance flows rivers of
living water to water the parched land around you.
Look and see, for the world is truly thirsty
for all that I have to give them.
Tell them I love them.

John 8:47

"He that is of God hears God's words..."

TOUCH OTHERS LIVES

I have new things for you to do to stretch
your faith.
Have I not said I will equip you to do the things I
call you to do;
and give you the words to speak?
Yes, I say, go forth and as you go where
I lead you, in your every day things, you will
influence the lives of others as I desire
you to do so.
Trust in Me whenever you question
anything I ask of you;
for you can do all things through the power that
dwells in you through My Holy Spirit.
A quiet time from every day "stuff" is
very important.
Time away from the things of this world,
to enter into My presence.
This takes discipline and concentration.
You thoughts must be turned to Me fully in order
to hear what I need to say to you.
I long to speak with My people, as I did in times past.
Draw near to Me,
and I will draw near to you.

Psalms 139:23+24

"Search me, O God, and know my heart: try me, and know my thoughts: And see if there be any wicked way in me, and lead me in the way everlasting"

TRUE SURRENDER

Did I not tell you, you are in the battlefield of life?
My Spirit leads you into prayer.
You must come before Me early to set your day in order.
Remember though, that the battle is not yours,
the battle belongs to the Lord, your God.
Spend time in My Word and the Holy Spirit will
teach you all things.
The joy of the Lord is your strength.
Your peace and joy is restored as you spend with Me.
Yes, you have heard and you know, yet
you have not applied the time to listen.
A meek and quiet spirit is one in which I can impart wisdom.
The darts of the enemy are pointed at you because you are
My disciple.
Be alert, be on your guard. Build yourself up
continually in My Word
When things happen…stand back and watch.
Though difficult, do not interfere. Trust Me. Lean on Me.
Focus and remember that all things work
together for good for those who love Me and are
called according to My purpose in Christ Jesus.
There's a reason for everything.
Be quiet and listen to those around you.
Let stuff be, watch and focus on what I will do.
Let go and turn everything and
everyone over to Me, including yourself.
Surrender all.
I will restore the joy of your salvation and
renew a steadfast spirit within you.

Ephesians 1:13+Deuteronomy 28:2

"In Whom ye also trusted, after that ye heard the Word of Truth,
the gospel of your Salvation; in whom also, after that ye believed,
ye were sealed with that Holy Spirit of promise."
"And all these blessings shall come on
thee, and overtake thee,
if thou shalt harken unto the voice
of the Lord thy God."

TRUST AND OBEY

Trust and obey, for there's no other way to be happy
in Jesus, than to trust and obey.
This little song with a strong message kept coming
to my mind today. I asked God, no other way?
Here was His answer to me, as I took my pen in hand…
From the beginning of a person's spiritual walk, a trust
arose in their heart.
They heard My Word and trusted it to be Truth,
which brought forth a desire to accept
My Great Salvation!
They saw My blood that was shed for them as
a new beginning, which was the very purpose of
My death and resurrection.
I did it all for you.
A believer who trust Me with their lives,
also desire to obey Me, the Author and finisher
of their faith.
I not carry them through all difficulties life brings?
Put no trust in yourself, for without Me, you can do nothing.
Allow My Holy Spirit within you to guide all that you do.
Cling to the body of Christ I place you in;
that you may continue to learn and grow in the
knowledge of your Lord and Savior, and the grace
which I bestow upon you.
Trust and obey that you might experience the
joy and peace I, alone, can give you.

Psalm 62:8

"Trust in Him at all times; ye people, pour out your heart before Him: God is a refuge for us."

TRUST GOD'S TIMING

Yes, I put things on your heart, then I show you
how to wait on Me
For then you will see how I bring things to pass.
I long to show you the way to the abundant life
I have promised you.
As you humble yourselves, you will then see
My hand in everything you do;
experiencing the leading of My Spirit.
You may not understand all, This is how I am glorified.
You allow Me to work in and through you
as you yield to My will by faith.
I open doors that seem impossible to open for you.
I close doors when I see danger of you walking
out of My will.
Yet, you can still choose to open and close the same
doors at your own will, if you do not wait for
My guidance.
When you feel the peace that passes all understanding,
you will know exactly what you will need to do.
Do not hurry ahead of Me.
Let Me show you the way to walk in this life;
and you will find that peace in all you do.
Wait on Me, I say, and see what glorious
things I will do for you.
I am a blessing God and desire to bless you
in every way.
The more you give of yourself to Me,
the more blessings I will bestow upon you.
Comfort yourself in this, want nothing but what
I want for you, and see the windows of heaven
open unto you.

John 8:32

"Ye shall know the truth, and the truth shall make you free."

TRUTH

I know your heart. It is ever bent towards
pleasing Me.
I will not let you fall, when you ask for My
keeping power.
Yes, life is full of decisions; and you come to the
source of power within you that leads
and guides you into all truth.
Life is difficult only when you do not desire
My will—Let Go—enjoy what and who
I bring into your life. Let Me bless you.
Do not fear what man can do to you.
Will I not protect you as I always have?
Whenever you surrender your will to Mine,
you will have peace.
Ah, yes, I give you choices.
Otherwise you wouldn't learn to use the
faith I have given you, to know what is My
best for you.
Walk in truth and honesty, and you will
find strength. You convictions will be strengthened.
I am a God of love, so let My love flow through you.
Be who I made you to be.
Rest in Me and know that I am always doing a
new thing in you.
Walk by faith, not by sight, and you will
fulfill My calling for you.
Do not try to understand with the human
mind, but with excitement and joy
receive by faith all that I bring you,
for My purpose and glory.

Philippians 2:13

"For it is God which works in you both to will and to do of His good pleasure."

VESSEL OF HONOR

Have I not promised to meet all your needs according to My riches in
Christ Jesus? I work all things together for good for those
who love Me and are called according to My purpose.
Being worked out in the power of My Son's Name; by My
Holy Spirit dwelling in and flowing through you.
All things are possible with Me, I am the God of all Creation.
Yet you must step out in faith and speak the Word of Truth
that I may be glorified.
My people hold back My glory, at times, because of their unbelief.
Whatever you ask in My Son's name and according to
my will, I will do.
Be My willing vessel. You will see the fruit of you
faithfulness.
You will see my hand in everything you do, for you have
realized, apart from me, you can do nothing.
Go forth with confidence, for I go before you, I am
with you, and I prepare the way for you.
I desire to set people free when they heed to My Truths that
you speak to them.
Time with me is essential. How can anyone truly experience
the blessings of God, lest they come before Me and
receive from Me.
I long to make Myself known to My people who humble
themselves to pray and spend time in My presence.
You are precious in My sight.

Daniel 12:3

"They that be wise shall shine as the brightness of the firmament;
And they that turn many to righteousness as the
Stars for ever and ever."

VICTORY IS YOURS

Ah, another corner in the road of life to get around.
Is anything too difficult for the God of your Salvation?
Keep focused on "the big picture".
Everyone has their own trials to bear. Remember…
I have a purpose for everything. Always wait on Me, and
watch what I will do. I will never leave you nor forsake you.
You have learned that yourself and others have
let you down many times.
Yet, haven't I picked you up again and helped you move on?
Be of a quiet spirit, as I help you endure other's afflictions
and "be there" for them.
There is much going on with the people around you,
yet you are able to experiencing My peace.
The joy of the Lord is your strength. There is no need to
fret about circumstances, when you surrender them
to My will.
Situations will come and go, I will remain steadfast
and guide your steps.
With confidence you will walk the path I have set before you.
The people in your life are there to share
and continue to learn of Me.
Much is required of my disciples; you must rely on Me fully.
Your faith in Me will always be your fortress in any storm.
Victory is yours…, your God, has already fought
the battle for you, and you are the winner!

Proverb 3:5

"Trust in the Lord with all thine heart; and lean not
unto your own understanding.
In all thy ways acknowledge Him,
and He will shall direct thy paths."

WAIT AND SEE

Do whatever you have to do to keep your serenity.
Do not be concerned about what others are doing.
Concentrate on what I, your God am doing.
Learn and then learn more.
This way you will understand even more why My people
need me in there lives.
This is not a game, it is life.
Haven't I always given you a way of escape from
those who trouble you and continue to create discord
for the brethren?
Wait and see what I will do.
Remember I am leading you, even though at times
it may seem contrary to My usual instructions.
I do not change, people do.
Through My Holy Spirit you will do and say things
you may not fully understand,
but you will see the fruit
of your obedience in time.
"Trust and obey—for there's no other way
to be happy in Jesus just trust and obey."
This is the way, walk ye in it.

Romans 8:25

"But if we hope for that we see not,
then do we with patience wait for it."

WAIT PATIENTLY

Much is happening in your life right now—change—
our human nature rebels against change;
yet spiritually we are crying out for it.
In the flesh we are nothing apart from Christ.
God in you, the hope of glory.
I have placed you in the world for My purpose
to be fulfilled in and through you.
Will I not set you free from the burdens that hold
you bondage to this world?
What you have committed to Me, I will take care of.
I will never let you down. I know your needs
and I will meet them.
I hear the cry of your heart and I will answer.
Do I not change your desires to follow My will?
Yes, and I lead and guide you in all things.
Decisions and change are not easy for the human nature,
that is why you must feed your spirit.
Your faith will grow stronger as you wait and see
how I bring all to pass.
I desire you to be free from burdens, so your mind
and heart can truly be centered on Me and
My calling for your life.
I will use your experience and maturity for
My glory and praise.
Wait patiently and see what awaits you. I love you.

Psalm 27:14

"Wait for the Lord; be of good courage,
and He shall strengthen thine heart:
wait, I say, on the Lord."

WALK BY FAITH

Am I your God who desires to bless you,
meet your needs,
answer your prayers and direct your path?
I tell you wait, see and watch for My hand to guide you;
and you will see My will unfold for you once again.
I want and know what is best for you.
I bring everyone into your life for my purpose.
You are mine.
I work ALL things together for your good,
because you love me.
Walk, by faith, the path I have chosen for you.
You need not fear the course your life is taking right now.
I mean it for good and not to harm you.
You have learned, my child, that in this world there are
those who mean to harm you, but I will always protect you.
I have also brought those to you who you can trust.
Lean on them, they love you as I love you, unconditionally.
You know who they are, for your heart is telling you.
Go forth into a new refreshing, receiving the blessings
I have set before you.
Know and experience My love in a new dimension.

1 Corinthians 14:33

"For God is not the author of confusion,
but of peace, as in all churches of the saints."

WALK IN CONFIDENCE

There are so many ways My people choose to go;
many things they choose to do, not even knowing if any of
these choices are My will for them.
The only way to know My will and to walk in it, is
to come before Me humbly submitting all to Me.
Then you will experience the peace that passes all
understanding; acknowledging that all is in vain that is
not done through My Spirit.
My anointing is necessary for you to accomplish
anything for Me, your God.
It is very sad to see My people walking in the insecurity
of the flesh, knowing it is not My way for them.
My way gives you confidence to choose to walk in the Spirit.
The flesh is weak, but My Spirit is strong.
My way is easy, not frustrating nor destructive.
My way is not grievous unto you, it is peaceful
and easily accepted.
For you are no longer in control, I am, when You allow
Me to be Lord of your life.
In all things through prayer and petition you can make
your requests know unto Me, and I will bring it to pass.
I am the author and finisher of your faith.
This is the way, walk ye in it.
Then the flesh will experience peace and will not
have dominion over the Spirit who dwells in you.

2 Corinthians 12:9

"And He said unto me, My grace is sufficient
for thee: for My strength is made perfect in weakness."

WALK IN HIS POWER

The human nature doubts and fears, but with
your God all things are possible.
There is nothing I can't do.
All I ask is for My people to be willing
vessels for Me.
In My name you will go forth and proclaim
the Good News that I live in the heart of men who receive
My forgiveness and salvation.
I move through surrendered lives.
You can only move and minister to others when
you are totally surrendered and relying on Me to
direct your path daily.
I called men and women of old to be My disciples.
Why would I not call you?
Oh, you say, you are not worthy or adequate.
Your Father in heaven has promised to
equip you with all you need to do His work here
on earth.
He has already given you all the gifts and talents
with which to use you for His glory.
You, by faith must go forth as the doors
of opportunity open to you.
For I will open the windows of heaven for you
to accomplish what I have planned and purposed
for you to do.
Walk in faith and in the power of My Holy Spirit.
Doing a new thing for, and in, and to thee glory
and praise of our Almighty God.

Psalm 119:105

"Thy Word is a lamp unto my feet,
and a light unto my path."

WALK IN THE LIGHT

Are you recognizing how and when I bring you through
difficult situations?
Every step you take and each person you have contact with
is ordained by Me; even the air you breathe.
When you expect Me to intervene for you and
look for Me, then you will see My purpose fulfilled.
So many times My people will never move unless there
be a crisis that moves them.
This ought not to be…move as I guide you.
You need never question why or how things are happening.
Seek My will and allow Me to do the things I need to do to
bring all to pass.
My way is always the best for you.
Trust Me, do not let circumstances discourage you.
Know that I am in the midst of your activities.
Be mindful of my presence continually.
I want to renew your faith, and encourage you on
your spiritual journey.
If My people will not hear Me, I am not able to guide them.
You will walk to and fro with no direction and no
purpose in life.
I have called you out of darkness into My marvelous LIGHT.
When you cannot see your way, WAIT on the Lord and
HE will see you through.
Trust and obey, for there's no other way,
to be happy in JESUS than to TRUST and OBEY!

1 John 4:15+16

"Whosoever shall confess that Jesus is the
Son of God, God dwells in him, and he in God."
"And we have known and believed the love that
God hath to us. God is love;
and he that dwells in love dwells in God,
and God in him."

WALK IN THE SPIRIT

All that you do, do as unto Me, your Savior.
It is good to be busy about your Father in Heaven's business.
Going to and fro, helping others around you;
being mostly concerned with their spiritual needs.
Spreading the good new that Jesus lives, and
desires to live in the hearts of men through His Holy Spirit.
There is nothing more important in these days
than encouraging folk to surrender to the will
of their Heavenly Father.
He, alone, knows what is best for them.
He created and knows what He purposed
for your life.
Yet few there be who earnestly seek after
God's perfect will.
You see, I will not force My will on anyone.
I desire for you to surrender your will, in order
to have My direction in your life.
Come unto Me, and I will give you rest for your
weary souls.
Nothing is too difficult for Me, no problem too big.
I am your All Mighty God.
Give Me your complete trust, for I will`
never let you down.
I will raise you to new dimensions in
the Spirit, as you walk with Me.

Joshua 24:15+23

"And if it seem evil unto you to serve the Lord, choose you this day whom you will serve; Now therefore put away the strange gods which are among you, and incline your heart unto the Lord God of Israel."

WALK IN TRUTH

My people will never be free as long as they yield themselves
to the wiles of the devil and the temptations of this world.
The flesh longs for the passions of sin.
I, your Lord, says to you: If you will humble yourself
and pray and seek only My will for you;
then will I give you overcoming power from the
bondage of sin that tries to rage in you.
You must desire freedom from all sin or you
will stay captive to it.
You must be sincere for I know the thoughts and intents
of your heart.
Be not deceived, for your adversary, the devil, prowls
around seeking whom he may devour.
He is working all the time to trap you and cause
you to fall away from Me and My purpose for your life.
Do you not know, he comes to rob and destroy all I have
to give you?
Sin separates you from Me; be not entangled with
a yolk of bondage.
Be mindful as you seek to fulfill the desires your
flesh cries out for; that this is sin against your Heavenly Father.
There is nothing your flesh craves that glorifies Me.
That is why you must worship Me with your body,
soul, and spirit.
Walk in truth and be not caught up in the lies
of Satan; and allow passions of this world and flesh
creep in and justify them as okay. You know right from wrong.
You know the truth, walk in truth, and
the truth shall make you free.

John 8:12

"Then spake Jesus again unto them, saying,
I am the light of the world:
he that followeth Me shall not walk in darkness,
but shall have the Light of Life."

WALK THE WALK

You are My child, I am your heavenly Father.
I have chosen you from the beginning and you
have seen the light.
Acceptance of My way is the way to freedom.
All bondage must flee.
A surrendered vessel is no longer bound, but
free from the chains of slavery.
Free to choose who you will serve each minute
of each day.
You can now have confidence of My direction for your life.
I will guide you into all truth.
My Word is your daily guide.
As I have led My people in the past, so shall I lead you.
I desire to use you to touch the lives of those I
bring into your life.
You are a living epistle when you seek My word
to know Me and the power of My resurrection.
Resurrection power, victory over sin, bondage and death!
Come forth and walk in newness of life, for the
God of your salvation sets you free.
Walk in that freedom, stand fast in the liberty
given you at the Cross.
Others will see what I want them to see in you;
as you walk the walk I have purposed especially for you.
Continue to spend much time with Me, in My Word
to learn of Me and My light will shine forth
from you.
As you lift Me up, I will draw all men unto Me.

Philippians 4:6

"Be anxious for nothing, but in everything by prayer and supplication with thanksgiving, let your requests be made known unto God."

WATCH AND PRAY

Talk with Me as you would a friend, knowing and
expecting Me to respond.
I desire to be intimate with My people.
As you have experienced, you must be ready to listen.
Much is going on around you, but be anxious for nothing.
Be careful to allow My Holy Spirit
to lead you in every situation.
Remember there are people involved in your life
wherever you go.
What you do influences them as well as yourself.
That is why it is so important to seek Me first,
that you may have the confidence that I am directing your path.
There is always choices in life, yet there is only
one right choice in every decision to be made.
When you seek My will, I will give you peace in the direction
you should go.
My way is not grievous unto you, but pleasant and easy.
For the door will open for you to walk through,
or close if need be. You are going to see many more things
that you desire to do for Me come to pass.
Watch and pray as I show you My plans.
Lives around you will be changed as you bring them before Me
in prayer.
Wait on Your Lord in great expectation, for
what you ask I will do.
In My time and for My glory.
Let faith direct your every move.

Philippians 4:7

"And the peace of God, which passes all understanding,
shall keep your hearts and minds in Christ Jesus."

WATCH, PRAY AND EXPECT

The end of another month and the beginning of
new things
I am doing in your life.
A new spiritual dimension to step into, as you learn to
leave others with me.
Letting go when all other instincts say do something.
This is one of the most difficult things I ask
of My people.
You need to let go, so I can intervene.
You may be in My way, doing your thing.
Stand back, I say, watch, pray and expect.
There are so many who are stubborn.
The do not realize they are powerless
without Me.
Comfort yourself in the knowledge that I will
never leave you; I am with you always,
You can handle more when you are trusting me
completely.
Though others around you are troubled, you will
experience peace.
This is the peace that passes all understanding.
Some will think you don't care; but
again it is because they do not understand.
All things are done for their own good.

2 Timothy 2:15

"Study to show thyself approved unto God,
a workman that needs not to be ashamed,
rightly dividing the Word of Truth."

WELCOME MY PRESENCE

Look around you, busy people everywhere.
No time for Me, their God, especially
to get quiet enough to hear Me.
Yet, I must tell you as your mind is stayed
on Me, then in all situations, at all times you are
in tune to My voice.
My Spirit speaks with your spirit and
directs your path.
My still small voice is heard among the
other voices and noises around you.
This is because you submit yourself to Me
in the early hour and ask that I have My way.
Yes, things get in your way or they don't seem to
go along as planned or expected,
Nothing in this life really matters, but My will.
Don't sweat the small stuff.
As you go along in life with a desire to serve
Me and obey Me, then
All will work together for your good,
You are My child and I to desire bless you.
I also require much of you.
Your quality time with Me is essential;
to know Me and the power of My resurrection.
To learn of Me and My ways by faithfully and
devotedly reading My Word.

Hebrews 6:11

"And we desire that every one of you do show the same diligence
to the full assurance of hope unto the end."

WITH ALL DILIGENCE

There is never a time that you will not find Me.
It is important for you to come aside and spend time
in My presence.
Meditate on the things you are learning of Me, as
My Way becomes an intricate part of your life.
You way never works, walk your own way,
do your own thing and you will fail.
All must be done decently and in order.
To be diligent in obeying Me in all situations, you must
continually learn My ways.
Even the minor details of life must be submitted to Me
to help you with.
I require your ALL, totally surrendered; otherwise
self will want to dominate and control to make
things go Your way.
This is a selfish generation. Selfishness destroys
My love flow. Think before you speak.
What would I, your God say? What would I do?
I promise always to help you respond in the Spirit
when you submit to Me and rely on Me.
Look not to your own understanding, obey.
Listen for the prompting of My Holy Spirit always.
If you do not recognize My prompting, then
wait quietly and listen for it.
No matter who you are with, listen, for they may
speak what I want you to hear.
Know I am in your midst, waiting to intervene that
My will and purpose be done in all situations.
Stand fast, yield, watch and see.
I am the Great I AM; and I will see you through
to the abundant life I promise those who walk with Me.

John 4:24

"God is a Spirit:
and they that worship Him
must worship Him in spirit and in truth."

WORSHIP ME

There are so many ways to worship Me.
The best way is with simplicity of heart.
Desiring to be with Me, dwelling in My presence,
filled with My Spirit.
To be full means to be overflowing with the Power
of My Holy Spirit.
Others will know that you have spent time
in My presence.
Who you spend time with, you become like.
The more you learn of Me and My ways, the more
spiritually mature you become.
My way for you is not burdensome, but
light and full of blessings.
All around you, you experience answered prayer.
For when you ask, believing, you will receive.
All things come from Me.
Be confident in all that I ask you to do in My name.
Know that I have put within you all that is
needed to fulfill the task.
It isn't what and how you perform.
It is by My Spirit that all is accomplished.
Be not discouraged if some do not respond.
Know that My Word will not return void.
I will be glorified whenever you step out
for My glory.
Your life is hid in Me. Nothing else matters,
but seeking My will and purpose in every way;
spreading My Word to this dying world.

Philippians 2:13

"For it is God which works in you both to will and to do of His good pleasure."

WORSHIP

There are so many ways you can worship Me.
On the street, in a store, in your neighborhood.
All those you meet will know you have been in My presence.
When you walk in the Spirit you do not fulfill the lusts of the flesh. Your will becomes My will, when you want My direction for your life.
I will show you the way.
So many changes, but aren't they all for the better?
Life is full of change, but I, your Lord, never change.
I care for you and will direct you steps.
I promise you an abundant life.
That life is only found in Me.
Be saturated in the things of God' enjoy the pleasures I bestow on you on the earth.
Draw close to those who love you; for this life is short and I have given you people you cherish and love.
You will give to each other wisdom and instruction through Me.
Life's experiences happen with my people as they draw their hearts together. I am in their midst.
I will teach, instruct, and admonish when you are together in My Name.
I draw you closer to each other and to Me.
Look to the changes that come to you, and learn from them. You will grow in the knowledge of your Lord Jesus Christ as you move, live and have your being in and through His Spirit.
LOVE ONE ANOTHER

Isaiah 30:21

"And thine ears shall hear a word behind thee,
saying, This is the way, walk ye in it,
when ye turn to the right hand, and
when ye turn to the left."

YOU ARE CHOSEN

So often you call on Me now with great
expectation in your heart.
There is no hesitation in knowing I will
speak with you. This is how it should be.
I will not let you down nor disappoint you.
Coming to Me in humbly will increase your faith.
You will become more and more sensitive to
My still soft voice.
My sheep hear My voice and they follow Me.
This produces true obedience to My
divine direction for your life.
There are many voices in this world.
You must take time to listen for Mine.
I can and will direct you in other ways also,
but listening to Me is the most intimate way
is to know Me.
When we commune together, we are the closest
we can be in this earthly realm.
Draw close to God and He will draw close to you.
Come away My beloved, and search the deep
recesses of your being. You belong
to the Almighty God;
for you have chosen to accept My Son, Jesus Christ
as your personal Lord and Savior.
I have an awesome plan for you. Be patient and flexible,
knowing and desiring to fulfill your God given calling.
For I know the way in which you should go…
all you need to do is walk in it.

Proverb 16:3

"Commit thy works unto the Lord, and
thy thoughts shall be established."

YOU ARE MY VESSEL

You will have peace whenever I am leading you.
There will be no question in your heart as to what you need to do.
Many find themselves in difficult circumstances because
they have put themselves there. Running with no real direction,
with the enemy forcing them down his path of destruction.
How can you help them, if I, your God can't?
They do not seek Me. I ask you to turn their focus to me.
For without Me they will fail.
When self is on the throne of a life, then I cannot be.
I desire to direct your steps, yet many choose to walk alone.
Then they wonder why nothing works out.
Remember, I have a reason and purpose for everything.
I created you. I know you better than you know yourself.
I not know what is best for you.
Stand back and wait on Me, after you have delivered My Truth.
Trust in Me for I have told you of the ways I will use you.
You may not understand or see the fruit for a time.
Yet My Word never returns void.
A seed planted will bring forth fruit in time,
depending on the soil in which it was planted.
Your only concern and responsibility is to be obedient in
speaking forth My Truth, not how or if it is received.
Remember, there were those who came against Me;
shall things be any different with you who
bring forth My Word?
You are my vessel, I know how I want to use you.
You just know and believe in Who I Am
and continue to speak my Truths to all
who will listen.

CPSIA information can be obtained
at www.ICGtesting.com
Printed in the USA
LVHW051405050522
717952LV00003B/116

9 781958 122280